We are delighted to pay tribute to Her Majesty The Queen on this very special occasion, the 70th anniversary of her accession to the Throne. We wish her the greatest of health and happiness as she marks this historic milestone. For all of us, this unprecedented Platinum Jubilee is an opportunity to celebrate the extraordinary service of The Queen and the role she has played in the world at large.

It is also an opportunity as a publisher to showcase the fascinating archive material from The Illustrated London News and its sister titles, documenting The Queen's reign over 70 years. From her early years as a child and young Princess, through to the Coronation and her adult life as Queen, wife, mother, grandmother and great-grandmother, we have compiled a breathtaking selection of unseen and rarely viewed images from our archives.

Wishing a joyous Jubilee to all our readers,

LISA BARNARD
Chief Executive
Illustrated London News Limited

Top: The Illustrated London News celebrates the royal tour of 1953
Left: Queen Elizabeth II with her son Prince Charles in 1953

The *Illustrated Platinum Jubilee* is published by **Illustrated London News Limited**, Coppergate House, 10 Whites Row, Spitalfields, London E1 7NF, U.K. Tel: +44 (0) 207 426 1011. www.iln.co.uk

Editor
Caroline Frost

Art Director
Dee Iva

Group Advertising Manager
Jane Washbourn
tel: +44 (0) 7920 821577
email: jane.washbourn@iln.co.uk

Director of Partnerships & Digital Marketing
Sophie Stoneham
email: sophie.stoneham@iln.co.uk

International Sales Director
Victoria Stringer

Advertising Sales Manager
David Allard

Production Director
David Gyseman

Chief Executive
Lisa Barnard
tel: +44 (0) 207 426 1011
email: lisa.barnard@iln.co.uk

All images in *The Illustrated Platinum Jubilee* are from The Illustrated News archive at Mary Evans Picture Library, unless otherwise stated.

www.maryevans.com
tel: +44 (0) 20 8318 0034

Pre Press by: Zebra
Printed by: Precision Colour Printing
Distribution: Seymour Distribution Ltd

THE ILLUSTRATED
Platinum Jubilee

THE ROYAL BRIDE

COLOURISED PHOTOGRAPH BY DOROTHY WILDING FOR THE ILLUSTRATED LONDON NEWS
PUBLISHED 29 NOVEMBER 1947

CONTENTS

CHAMPAGNE

BOLLINGER

MAISON FONDÉE EN 1829

HER MAJESTY'S PLATINUM PLEDGE

As our Queen celebrates this milestone unmatched in a thousand years of British monarchy, Caroline Frost reflects on the majesty of a royal who never expected to reign

For anybody to spend 70 years in a single role is an achievement worthy of notice. For the Queen to have reached her Platinum Jubilee and to enjoy unprecedented levels of respect, affection and personal popularity among her subjects is nothing short of extraordinary.

As we raise our glasses to toast this remarkable milestone, we can reflect that this is our great fortune as much as it is the Queen's. In an era of unpredictable politics, economic challenges, and social and cultural change, we have in our monarch a beacon of integrity and constancy that we have never appreciated more.

We are lucky too that the fates conspired nearly a century ago to thrust this ordinary, unassuming woman into a unique position, and that her personal qualities enabled her to meet responsibilities she could not have dreamed of in her earliest years.

For her first decade, young Princess Elizabeth's childhood, background and tastes appeared to set her safely on a path of aristocratic but homely life filled with family, animals and country pursuits. Instead, her uncle's abdication in 1936 meant her father, traumatically and unexpectedly, became King George VI, with his elder daughter first in line to the throne.

Even then, it seemed she could look forward to many years of fun, spending periods abroad as the wife of a naval

officer, bringing up her own family and supporting her beloved father when required.

Instead, another shocking brush with fate took her in another direction entirely. On 6 February 1952, the King died unexpectedly in his sleep at Sandringham, aged just 56.

Elizabeth was away on a trip she had taken on his behalf. On her way to Australia and New Zealand, she had stayed at the Treetops Hotel in Kenya the night before the news reached her. As the history books would note, she went up the tree a princess and came down a queen. She returned home to London two days later. As cameras recorded her walking down the steps of her plane, waiting to be greeted by her first Prime Minister Winston Churchill, it was clear her life had changed forever.

By then, the Queen had already used the occasion of her 21st birthday to make a solemn pledge to the people of the British Empire and Commonwealth: "I declare before you all that my whole life, whether it be long or short, shall be devoted to your service."

For the 70 years that have passed since she inherited the throne, Her Majesty has never wavered from that promise.

Trained and guided in her early years by her father, the Queen has clearly inherited his work ethic and devotion to duty. On the hundreds of occasions when her subjects have

expected her to be there, the monarch has simply shown up, whether it be the State Opening of Parliament, Trooping the Colour, Remembrance Sunday or any one of countless pageants and ceremonies – all of which, without the Queen to shake hands, make a speech and perform the necessary public duties, would somehow seem incomplete.

There has been hardly a single day in 70 years when she has not attended to her affairs of state, studied her official papers brought to her in distinctive red boxes, met representatives of organisations, presented honours and awards, sat down with political leaders and other members of government, sent telegrams of congratulation or sympathy, and replied to the thousands of letters she has received from all over the world. In her 10th decade, she remains the patron of more than 600 organisations across the UK and Commonwealth.

As well as her duties at home, the Queen has kept herself accountable to her hundreds of millions of subjects worldwide, even as this number has depleted through the course of her reign, with Empire giving way to Commonwealth and many British territories moving towards independence. Through decades of change and political flux across the world, Her Majesty's presence abroad has done much to ease delicate relations between nations. She has visited an estimated 110 countries, and in return offered Britain's unique brand of regal hospitality to world leaders and

Above: The Duchess of York with her daughters Margaret and Elizabeth at the Aboyne Highland Games, 1946

Right: The first official wedding photograph of Princess Elizabeth and Philip Mountbatten, 20 November 1947

Above: The Queen returns from Kenya after the death of her father, King George VI, 7 February 1952
Right: Sisters Elizabeth and Margaret in pantomime, 1942
Below: Princess Elizabeth makes her 21st birthday broadcast to the Empire from South Africa, 1947
Opposite: The Queen and Duke of Edinburgh on the balcony at Buckingham Palace following Queen Elizabeth's first State Opening of Parliament, 1952

other dignitaries, contributing hugely to the United Kingdom's international standing.

At her side for her entire reign until last year was the Duke of Edinburgh. Along with her own temperament, one of the Queen's great strokes of good luck was to meet her lifelong companion when she was still very young. In Prince Philip, she found someone with whom she could share not just the burden of decades of public service, but also an enduring union of common personal interests and a rare mutual support.

It is one of the great paradoxes of our monarch that, while she is a living symbol of ancient majesty, she is also a daughter and a sister, a mother, a grandmother and a great-grandmother who presides over an ever-growing family, with all the delights and tribulations those roles bring.

It's probably fair to say that her blood relations have brought her trials to match any political or public challenges. Back in the 1950s, her sister Margaret famously dithered over whether to marry her divorced lover before finally deciding it couldn't happen. Then, during a tumultuous period in the 1990s, the Queen and Duke of Edinburgh could only look on as three of their four children were divorced, each bringing their own share of headlines. Even then, as she had done previously and has done ever since, Her Majesty said little in public and simply soldiered on with what she has always regarded as the main purpose of monarchy, that is to serve her people.

This resolve was perhaps most tested in 1997 when the death of Diana, Princess of Wales prompted outpourings of grief from the public. For the first time in her reign, the Queen found her own natural reserve out of kilter with the stronger emotions being expressed. Her decision to share her sadness at that time

was unprecedented but heralded a change in style by the entire monarchy that has served it well ever since.

While Her Majesty has naturally retained her elegance and dignity, she has in recent years developed a more open, accessible way of communicating with her subjects, whether that be taking part in a sketch with James Bond for the Opening Ceremony of the London Olympics, chatting to other Commonwealth leaders via the wonders of Zoom, or inspiring millions with personal messages during lockdown.

Allowing us to glimpse more of the person under the crown has inspired a fresh affection and appreciation for the Queen, to match the respect and admiration she has always enjoyed. In 2022, she remains as popular as at any time in her reign.

In our vibrant democracy, some will always debate the value of monarchy. But even the most ardent republican would agree that, in the monarch herself, we have someone who represents the best of Britain – devoted to her family, dedicated to her public and tireless in her purpose.

On 6 February 2022, the 70th anniversary of her accession to the throne, the Queen renewed the pledge she made all those years before, that her life would always be devoted to the service of her people – and she also thanked us. She said, "I remain eternally grateful for, and humbled by, the loyalty and affection that you continue to give me."

On this occasion of her Platinum Jubilee, while we toast both the quantity and quality of Her Majesty's unique reign, we must surely give thanks in return.

Above: The Duke of Edinburgh pays homage at the Coronation of Queen Elizabeth II, 2 June 1953

Left: The Queen cuts a cake at Sandringham to celebrate the start of the Platinum Jubilee

LALAGE BEAUMONT

READY-TO-WEAR, MADE TO MEASURE AND HANDBAGS

This page: Queen Elizabeth II, specially painted by Terence Cuneo for *The Illustrated London News* to celebrate the coronation, 1953

ANGOSTURA®

aromatic bitters

We wish Her Majesty good health and continued happiness

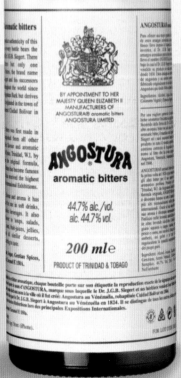

House of Angostura® offers its warmest congratulations to HM The Queen on the occasion of Her Majesty's Platinum Jubilee. ANGOSTURA® aromatic bitters is proud to hold a Royal Warrant of Appointment from HM Queen Elizabeth II since 1955.

a story in every dash

@ @houseofangosturaglobal

WHEN THE QUEEN COMES CALLING

The Queen has met probably more individuals than anyone else in history. Here, people from different walks of life describe how it feels when Her Majesty appears in person

ANN KENRICK
Master of the Charterhouse

"In early 2017, I took over as first female Master of the Charterhouse in London and one of my first challenges was to organise the opening of our museum and learning centre by the Queen, one of our royal governors. It was about a fortnight into my new job, so I had a few wobbles.

"We were really lucky that we had nice weather on the day. She arrived with the Duke of Edinburgh and they split up to talk to people. The Queen came with me to the learning centre where local young children were learning about heraldry, which meant designing their own coat of arms. I took her to meet some of the children, and what struck me was how interested she seemed in everything they were doing.

"She was very smiley and relaxed. Her warmth and sense of humour don't always come across on screen, but are very evident in person.

"We'd had a stone tile prepared to be opened by the Queen and Prince Philip, and my facilities team had gone out the night before to buy a curtain, which we'd had trouble attaching, so it was all hanging on with just a bit of Velcro.

"As we were walking towards it, I very quietly mentioned to the Queen, 'With the unveiling, sharp tug left to right, and then it will drop on the floor.' 'Fine,' she said. She just got it, and made no mention of the fact that we'd cobbled this curtain together at the last minute.

"The whole thing went very smoothly, and I thought, 'What a professional.' She's done it a million times, and she made everything very easy. I was incredibly grateful to her for making the first big task in my own job go off without a hitch."

GARETH MCLEAN
Writer

"This was a reception for young achievers at Holyroodhouse in Scotland, 1997. It was a big reception with everyone standing around, including members of the armed forces, charities and newcomers like myself.

"We were all told that the Queen would come round, and given the type of questions she would ask so we could prepare.

"Her Majesty seemed to glide in and started chatting. Earlier that day she'd opened The Scotsman's new building and also the presses down at Leith, which had a bit of a rough reputation back then. 'You were at my work today,' I told her. 'You're a brave woman going to Leith. I hope you kept hold of your handbag.'

"We both laughed and I affectionately touched her arm. You're not supposed to touch the Queen! It didn't faze her at all, but every head in the room swivelled round to stare. You can see us laughing as it was filmed and included in the Queen's Speech of that year. I only realised this when, five minutes after 3pm on Christmas Day that year, my phone went bananas."

ANDREW LANNERD
Historian and tour director

"In June 2006, I had the good fortune to be invited to a private garden party at Buckingham Palace. I was standing with a small group and the Queen walked across, waving her arms and saying, 'No more "happy birthdays". Everyone keeps wishing me happy birthday!' She was laughing, so I said, 'Well, Your Majesty, I hope you don't mind but I would like to add my best wishes for your birthday.' And she paused, and then with perfect comedic timing she replied, 'Well, okay, but you're the last one!' before letting out a huge laugh. She was great fun."

CHRIS WIMPRESS
Journalist

"I met the Queen in June 2013, when I was a duty editor of Radio 4's The World at One programme, and Her Majesty came to open the BBC's New Broadcasting House in central London.

"We were all told the day before that she would be coming, so everyone made an effort to dress more smartly than journalists usually do.

"Just before she arrived, I was on the phone at my desk. Suddenly, I realised that a sniffer dog was under my desk, happily eating the sandwich in my bag. It seemed that rather than looking for suspicious devices, the dog had decided it was time for lunch instead.

"When the Queen arrived, we all had to stand by our desks, and mine was right next to the printer. It's always very busy with all the Radio 4 news programmes, and it makes a huge noise. I was thinking, 'I hope nobody prints anything just as the Queen walks past.'

"It was very surreal to see her in person, walking along the line. When I saw her, I realised she's the same age and height as my grandmother, and I suddenly felt extraordinarily protective of her.

"I shook her hand, she smiled, then she was off to the studio to make her declaration and meet John Humphrys. I couldn't believe how quickly she moved, without ever seeming to be in a hurry.

"Newsrooms are very busy, loud places, but it seemed that for those few moments she was there, all the phones stopped ringing, and even the printer fell silent.

"It was a unique moment in an otherwise hectic newsroom."

RAYMOND EVISON
Former RHS Council member and Clemitis expert

"Because of my role at Chelsea, I've looked after Her Majesty during her visits on several occasions.

"She has a wide understanding of what is going on in the world. Her knowledge and her memory are both remarkable. When I received my OBE at Buckingham Palace, I was amazed that she had done her research and knew all about my history. I know she does this for everyone, but it is still a wonderful skill.

"About 15 years ago, I was invited to the palace for a reception for pioneers, with 300 people or so crowded into the hall, and the Queen was circulating and meeting us all. A group of us started talking about clematis and she said, 'I'd love to have clematis growing at Balmoral but sadly they won't be winter hardy enough.' I replied, 'Ma'am, with respect, I am sure they will be hardy enough.' As a result of that conversation, I was invited to go to Balmoral to advise on the clematis for the gardens. As far as I know, they've turned out very successfully, which is a relief. Whenever I met Her Majesty at Chelsea in the following years, we always talked about her clematis at Balmoral.

"I've met the Queen many times on public occasions, but it was very special for me to meet Her Majesty at Balmoral and to walk around her gardens, just the two of us. Because she was so relaxed, I relaxed as well, and I found her to be a wonderful person, kind and understanding. I felt elevated just talking to her. She is a very special person."

PIP JENKINS
Head designer, John Smedley, Royal Warrant holder

"In 2014, we had one day's notice that the Queen and the Duke of Edinburgh were coming to visit our factory and design studio – quite good in a way because it didn't give us much time to get nervous. We work next to the factory and normally you can hear the constant noise of machines, but they'd been turned off especially for the visit, so there was this eerie silence. As we all waited for the royal motorcade to arrive, you could have heard a pin drop.

"Our design team had prepared a presentation on our new-season collections, which the Queen seemed to be enjoying. Pretty soon, though, I noticed the Lord Lieutenant move up to her and suggest she might have to cut the show short so that they could stick to the timetable, as they were already running late.

"Fortunately, Her Majesty had other ideas. I noticed her smile at him but gently wave him away and then she carried on watching. I remember thinking, 'Phew, all is OK!' It really was such a relief. She watched until the end and then thanked everyone. There was such a buzz in the workshop for days afterwards, and because we're in the business, we particularly remembered her beautiful pale blue coat and hat. She looked immaculate, as always."

JASMINE FREEMAN
Festive well-wisher

"I have been to Sandringham at Christmas several times because my mum has to cover it for her work as a TV producer.

"The first year we went was in 2013, which was the last year that the Queen stopped to accept flowers from children. Since then, other members of the royal family have stayed behind after church to meet the public, but the Queen gets into her waiting car and goes back to Sandringham House.

"In December 2013, I was aged seven and very excited because I wanted to meet the Queen and give her flowers.

"We got to Sandringham very early in the morning and it was quite cold. We had to wait for a long time while the Queen was in church but, when she came out, the police invited the children in the crowd to come forward.

"I rushed to the queue to meet the Queen. I was near the back and started worrying she'd leave before I met her. When I reached the front, she wished me 'Merry Christmas' with a huge smile, and I gave her the flowers and curtsied. I was so happy and excited. It was a brief but special moment that will stay with me forever."

MORRIS BRIGHT MBE
Chair, Elstree Studios

"In the mid 1990s I was working as a press officer for a Member of Parliament, who asked me one week if I would like to attend a reception on his behalf. The event was to celebrate Commonwealth Day and Her Majesty the Queen was to be in attendance. He told me that there would be hundreds of people there and it was unlikely I'd get to see the Queen.

"There were indeed hundreds of people there. One of them turned out to be someone I knew well, a local religious minister, who had married my wife and me a few years before.

"As the Queen approached, he whispered, 'Come, stand with me, Morris.' There was an extraordinary aura around the Queen.

> "THERE WAS AN EXTRAORDINARY AURA AROUND THE QUEEN. I'D NEVER REALLY EXPERIENCED A FEELING QUITE LIKE IT"

I'd never really experienced a feeling quite like it. Her Majesty recognised my friend, stopped and started talking to him, then he said, 'Your Majesty, may I introduce a friend of mine who works in Parliament?' The Queen looked at me, smiled and asked me for whom I worked. When I explained it was Sir Colin Shepherd, well known for his Commonwealth work, she asked me to pass on her best wishes to Sir Colin. And then she moved on.

"I felt an extraordinary rush of adrenaline, like I had won an Olympic Medal or a BAFTA. It was extraordinary that one person could have such an effect, but the Queen did. She could probably see the nerves in my eyes, but she had a wide, comforting smile, lovely tone of voice and would clearly look at the person she was speaking to. For just that moment you were the only one in the room."

FROM
PRINCESS
TO
QUEEN

Young Princess Elizabeth enjoyed a carefree and peaceful childhood with her family in London and Windsor, providing a strong foundation for her unexpected future role

From the moment she came into the world on 21 April 1926, the young Princess Elizabeth was blessed with a fair complexion, a pair of brilliant blue eyes and, most importantly, a serene temperament that would serve her well.

Adored by her parents, doted on by her grandparents King George V and Queen Mary, surrounded by spoilt pets, Elizabeth knew only comfortable domesticity until 1936, when everything changed. That year saw the death of George V and accession of Edward VIII, until her Uncle David's shocking decision to abdicate meant her father was thrust reluctantly onto the throne, with Elizabeth next in line.

As the heir presumptive, the Princess supported the new King and Queen in boosting national morale during World War II, while she kept herself busy training as a mechanic with the Auxiliary Territorial Service. In peacetime, as Britain began to recover, the public were buoyed by news of the Princess's engagement to a dashing young lieutenant, Philip Mountbatten. The couple were married in November 1947, and soon started a family with the arrival of Charles in 1948 and Anne in 1950.

Opposite: Princess Elizabeth aged three in 1930
This page: Princess Elizabeth on the balcony at Buckingham Palace with her family; an early theatre outing; the princess helps walk her baby sister, Princess Margaret

Clockwise: Elizabeth and Margaret play with their corgis in their miniature Welsh cottage; 13-year-old Princess Elizabeth attends the Royal Naval College at Dartmouth with her sister and governess. It is there she meets her future husband Prince Philip of Greece; Elizabeth enjoyed a happy childhood with sister Margaret and their parents; the Princess in ATS uniform
Opposite: Princess Elizabeth enjoys a joke with her father King George VI

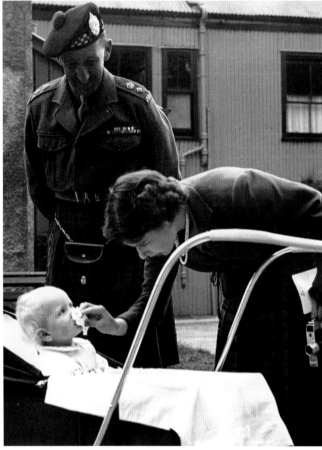

Clockwise: Elizabeth with her husband Philip during a visit to Malta, where the Duke was stationed as a naval officer, in 1950; the couple pose for an official photograph following their wedding at Westminster Abbey in November 1947; a Tatler cover features the Queen with her children Charles and Anne; the royal family wave off HM The Queen Mother at Waterloo in 1953; Princess Elizabeth tends her daughter Anne at Balmoral in 1951

JAN. 5
1955

Volume CCXV. No. 3251. TWO SHILLINGS.
Postage: Inland 1d. Canada 1½d. Foreign: 1½d.

The
TATLER
&
BYSTANDER

An inspiration for the New Year

THIS delightful portrait of the Queen with her children, Prince Charles and Princess Anne, is one of the happiest pictures for 1955. In the past year the affection in which Her Majesty is held personally has been strengthened throughout the Commonwealth by first-hand experience, and in her children, her subjects see reflected the happiness and tranquil home life of their own. With such mutual respect and understanding between ruler and people, the country enters upon the New Year with high confidence.

The Princess seemed set to enjoy many years of relatively normal adulthood, but the fates dealt another card on 6 February 1952. While Elizabeth and Philip were staying at the remote Treetops game lodge in Kenya during a trip to Africa that they had taken on behalf of her ailing father, the King passed away in his sleep at Sandringham. It was only when they moved on to their next stop that the Duke of Edinburgh received word and broke it to his wife that she now ruled over Great Britain and the Commonwealth. They immediately made plans to return to London, where Prime Minister Winston Churchill and other dignitaries were waiting to greet their new sovereign. Alone and upright, the young Queen walked down the aeroplane steps and into a brand new Elizabethan age.

The Queen's coronation was watched by 27 million people in the UK alone, and millions more across the world

EST · 1847

SEARCYS

LONDON

CONGRATULATIONS TO

Her Majesty The Queen

ON THE OCCASION OF
HER PLATINUM JUBILEE

Searcys has been
at the heart of
British hospitality
since 1847

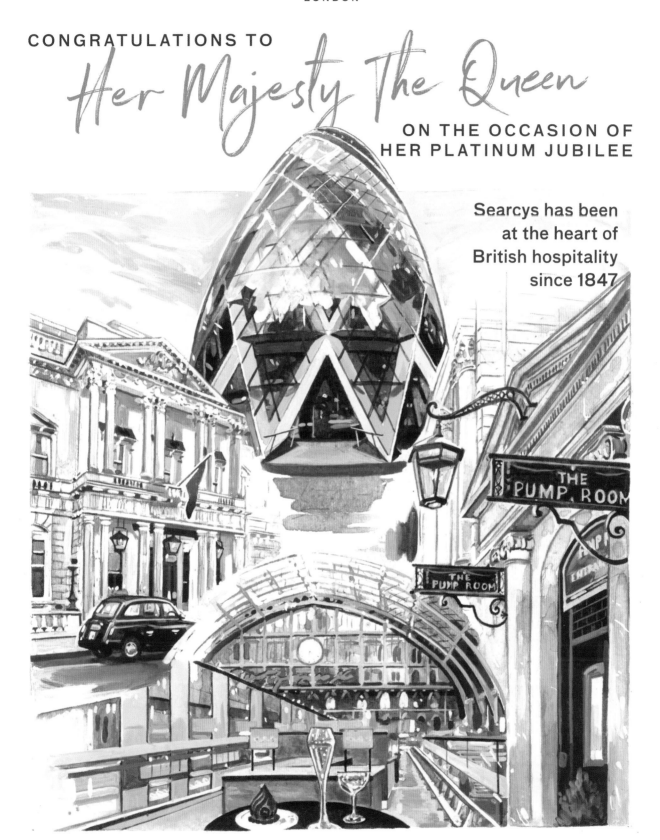

DISCOVER MORE

Searcys.co.uk

🐦 📷 f @SearcysLondon

SIGN UP TO WIN

A private dining experience
with Searcys

175 YEARS TOGETHER

The Queen and
Duke of Edinburgh
leave Westminster
Abbey following a
ceremony to mark
their silver wedding
Anniversary in
November 1972

1692

TAYLOR FLADGATE

TO HONOUR HER MAJESTY THE QUEEN'S 70 YEARS AS MONARCH,
TAYLOR'S PORT HAS BOTTLED A RARE TAWNY PORT.

A PERFECT WINE TO TOAST HER MAJESTY.

1692

TAYLOR FLADGATE

TAYLOR'S

VERY VERY OLD TAWNY PORT

TO COMMEMORATE
THE PLATINUM JUBILEE OF
HER MAJESTY QUEEN ELIZABETH II

ESTABLISHED IN 1692

BY APPOINTMENT TO
H.M. QUEEN ELIZABETH II
SUPPLIERS OF PORT WINE
TAYLOR'S PORT
PORTUGAL

TAYLOR.PT

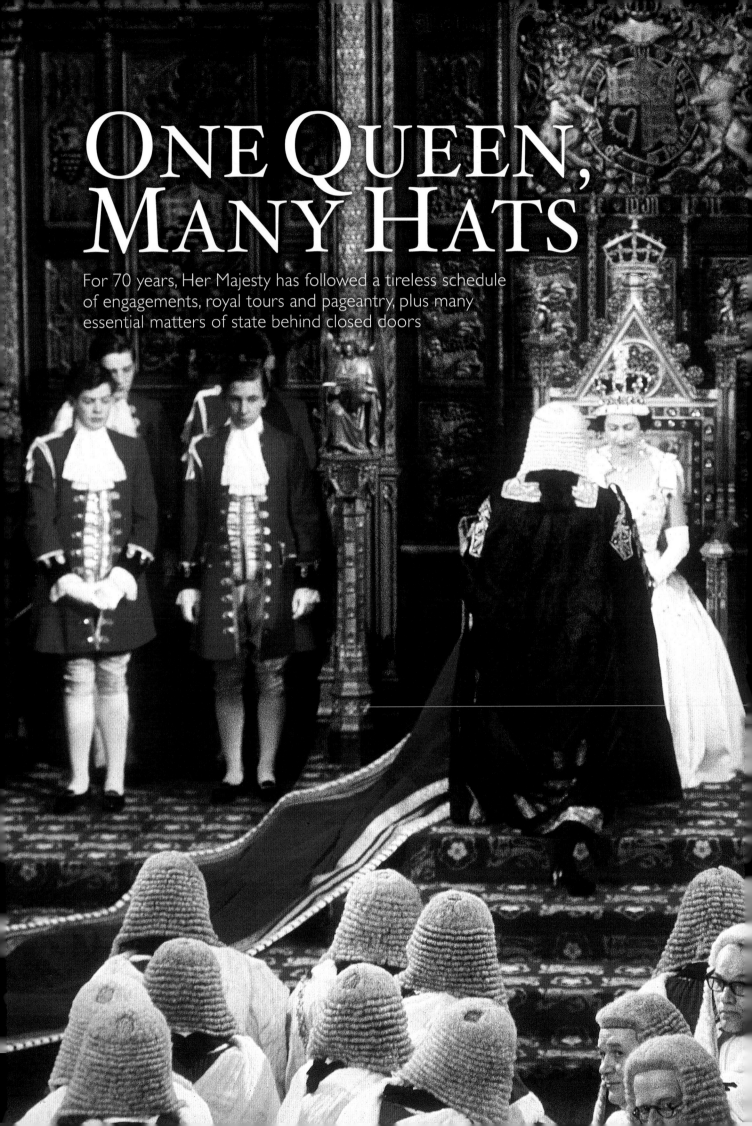

ONE QUEEN, MANY HATS

For 70 years, Her Majesty has followed a tireless schedule
of engagements, royal tours and pageantry, plus many
essential matters of state behind closed doors

Despite being born into it, the Queen sees the role of monarch very much as a job, and a serious one at that – a lifelong pledge of service, responsibility and a million duties, many of which are never seen by her public.

For a start there's all the pageantry which can't take place without her – the State Opening of Parliament, Trooping the Colour, and hundreds of dazzling banquets at either Buckingham Palace or Windsor Castle, where she plays host to political leaders from near and far, and an essential diplomatic role in her nation's relations with others.

Even when the diary is free of such glamorous events, the Queen's working week is full of appointments and meetings required to uphold her position as head of state – a catalogue of constitutional and representational duties that have evolved over a thousand years of history.

What does that look like from day to day? Well, first there are the famous red boxes, delivered punctually every evening in preparation for the following morning's work. Every day of the year, even if she does occasionally give herself a Monday off, the Queen spends between two and three hours attending to these piles of papers presented to her by her aides. Among them will be Foreign Office telegrams, the minutes from Cabinet Office meetings, and important memos from Departments of State, all needing her eye on them and, finally, her signature.

Then there are the appointments and honours. While these come via recommendations from government, they are made in her name and only the monarch can give them the official sign-off. In her 10th decade, the Queen remains the patron of more than 600 charities and organisations, for each of which any visit requires months of planning.

Left: Queen Elizabeth II in full regalia at the State Opening of Parliament, 1964
Above: Princess Elizabeth with US President Harry S Truman, 1951

While the Queen remains firmly politically neutral and must abide by democratic decisions made by Parliament, for 70 years she has met once a week with the British Prime Minister. For each of the 14 serving leaders she has sat down with in the course of her reign, the Queen is a fount of knowledge on current affairs, a rare source of wisdom in sometimes turbulent times and, of course, the soul of discretion.

She is also Defender of the Faith and Supreme Governor of the Church of England, requiring her to appoint its leaders, while acknowledging the multi-faith nation she represents.

Besides all her duties to Great Britain, Elizabeth II remains Queen of 14 other realms, so must keep herself thoroughly abreast of all information being imparted by those governments as well.

The Commonwealth has grown increasingly precious to the Queen, even as an increasing number of the countries within it move towards independence. An overseas visit by the monarch or members of her family can do wonders for foreign relations, and in return she ensures the best of hospitality for heads of state visiting the UK. Whatever the Queen feels privately about any individual either at home or abroad, very few will ever know. For her, a polite smile and a warm welcome are part of the job.

Clockwise from top: Arriving with the Duke of Edinburgh at Katunguru on a visit to Uganda, 1954; on a royal tour of the West Indies, 1966; the Queen and her 12th Prime Minister David Cameron at 10 Downing Street, 2012

The SPHERE
with which is incorporated THE GRAPHIC

Opposite page: Trooping the Colour, 1969

This page, clockwise from left: With then foreign minister Wu Xueqian on a state visit to China, 1986; working on state papers, 1959; the Queen and Duke of Edinburgh meet Pope John XXIII in Rome, 1961; horseriding with President Ronald Reagan at Windsor, 1982; with then French President Georges Pompidou at Versailles, 1972

The past decade, with the Duke of Edinburgh's final years, her own slowing down and more recently the challenges of lockdown, has inevitably seen the Queen begin to reduce her workload, passing her duties to other members of her family while remaining very much in charge. She has also taken clear pleasure in the advantages of modern technology to engage with her subjects near and far.

On 6 February 2022, the 70th anniversary of her accession to the throne, she renewed her pledge to devote her life to the service of her subjects. It was fitting that on the day she did this, the Queen was photographed at Sandringham with a familiar red box full of papers in front of her. It may have been a remarkable date in history but, for our monarch, it was equally just another day at the office.

Above: Feeding Donna the elephant at Whipsnade Zoo, 2017
Left: The Queen and Duke of Edinburgh being serenaded by the drums of the Orangemen outside Government House, Hillsborough, 1953

ALAMY

TOWN TALK

— POLISH CO LTD —

TOWN TALK
— POLISH CO LTD —
SILVER
POLISHING CLOTH
with anti-tarnish protection

TOWN TALK
POLISH CO LTD
PEARL
CARE KIT

TOWN TALK
— POLISH CO LTD —
SILVER
CUTLERY
RINSE
maximum strength

800ml ℮ 20.3FL OZ

TOWN TALK
— POLISH CO LTD —
JEWEL SPARKLE
liquid cleaner for
gold & precious stones

225ml ℮ 7.6FL OZ

Sparkling Since 1895®

The Queen and Duke at
Alice Springs, Australia, 1963

Arriving for a state
visit to Iceland, 1990

WHEN ONLY THE BEST WILL DO

As Her Majesty The Queen enjoys her Platinum Jubilee, premium chocolate-maker Bendicks, famous for its After Dinner Mints, celebrates its 60th year as a Royal Warrant holder

The Bendicks story began in 1930, when Mr Oscar Benson and Colonel Dickson started a small confectionery business on unassuming Church Street in Kensington, producing chocolates in a tiny basement beneath the store. A few years later, Bendicks was developing an enviable reputation for quality and a Bendicks store opened in the heart of London's exclusive Mayfair.

The rich and fashionable frequently visited the shop to enjoy the intense taste of a strong mint fondant, accompanied by 95% dark chocolate made from the finest cocoa beans. Known as the Bittermint, it was a phenomenon from the start and was to make Bendicks famous around the world.

The unrivalled reputation of Bendicks continued to grow and in 1962 Bendicks was awarded a Royal Warrant, "By Appointment to Her Majesty The Queen", a prestigious stamp of quality that has adorned every one of the beautifully distinctive chocolate boxes ever since. This year, Bendicks is honoured to celebrate the 60-year anniversary of holding the Royal Warrant.

Bendicks continues to build on its reputation and rich heritage, still paying the same attention to every detail at its factory as it did when the chocolates were made in a tiny basement beneath the shop in Kensington. Today, Bendicks is the premium after-dinner mint, delivering the perfect finishing touch to any meal or entertainment occasion.

Delivering the finest-quality chocolates has been achieved through the skill and artistry that has been passed down through the years. Bendicks has huge respect for traditional craftsmanship and is an avid supporter of The Queen Elizabeth Scholarship Trust, the charitable arm of the Royal Warrant Holders Association. This year marks the 10th year of the Bendicks scholarship for traditional craftsmanship.

Quality and tradition are fundamental to the longevity of the company's success. Bendicks looks forward to many more years of producing its famous chocolate mints and continuing to delight the most discerning customers.
www.bendicks.co.uk

GETTY

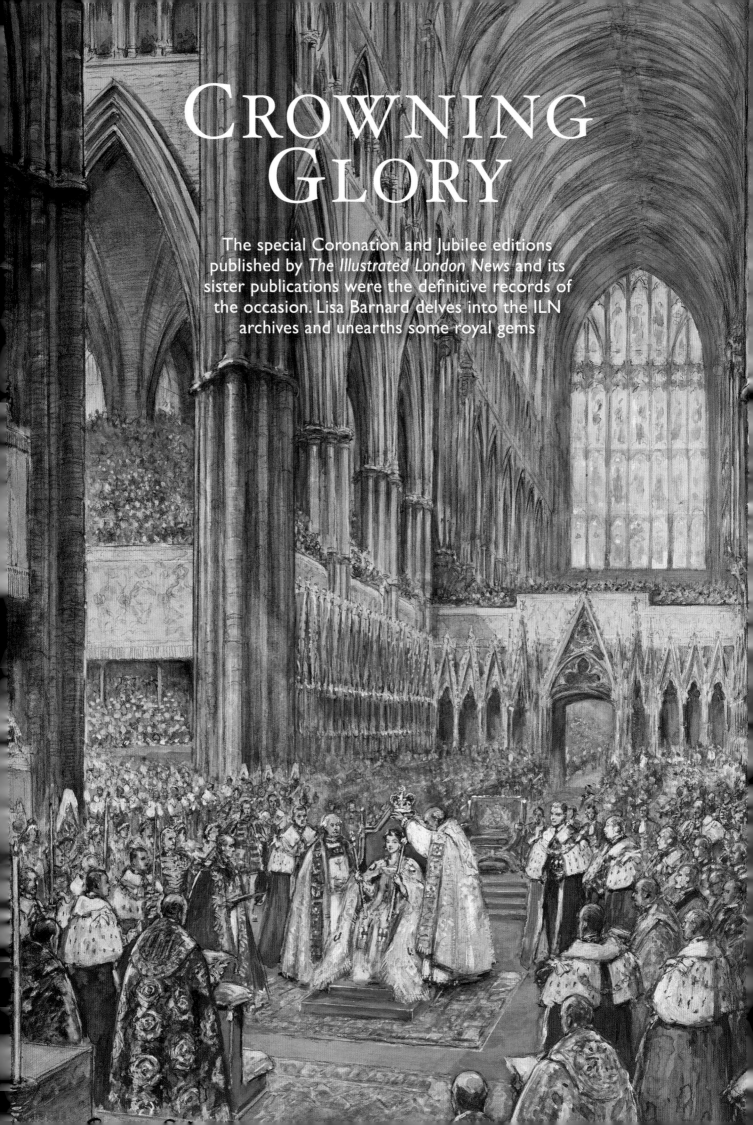

CROWNING GLORY

The special Coronation and Jubilee editions
published by *The Illustrated London News* and its
sister publications were the definitive records of
the occasion. Lisa Barnard delves into the ILN
archives and unearths some royal gems

There is no nation that knows how to stage a coronation quite like Britain, and in its heyday there was no publisher that knew how to turn out a coronation special edition better than *The Illustrated London News*. As the world's first pictorial magazine founded in 1842, marking a revolution in journalism and news reporting, just five years after Queen Victoria acceded the throne, the ILN proved that pictures sold and that great royal occasions – births, weddings, jubilees, funerals and above all coronations – were a publisher's dream. Unlike births, weddings and funerals, there is the benefit of advance notice between accession and the coronation ceremony, allowing the editorial team to go to town on preparing a coronation edition. In the case of Queen Elizabeth II, there was a generous interval of 16 months, allowing a traditional period of mourning for the passing of the previous monarch and for the planning committees to make their meticulous preparations.

The ILN commemorative royal editions set out to be the definitive record and a must-have collector's item: lavishly produced, bound with high quality covers, illustrated with exclusive commissioned portraits of the monarch, engraved decorative borders, in-depth articles and glorious colour plates of photographs capturing the monarch at all earlier stages of his or her life. The 1953 Coronation issue was no exception. The lead article, "The Record of the Life of Her Majesty Queen Elizabeth II" spanned some 30 pages and was written by the eminent historian and royal expert Sir Charles Petrie. It still reads today as an authoritative piece.

Opposite: The Coronation of Queen Elizabeth II in Westminster Abbey by Bryan de Grineau for the ILN
This page: A Day the World Remembers – Coronation scenes on 2 June 1953 in London

The edition also expounded the ritual and significance of the coronation in an article by the Dean of Westminster. This article was not as reverent as might be expected from the very Rev Dr A. C Don. He opens the article by describing the copy of the service used by Lord John Thynne, Canon and Sub-Dean of Westminster, on the occasion of Queen Victoria's Coronation. "Judging by the pencil notes scribbled in the margins after the conclusion of the ceremony, the proceedings appeared to be punctuated by considerable embarrassment and confusion." He recounts how the Bishop of Bath and Wells appeared to have turned over two pages of his book in error, and thus concluded that the Service was at an end. He announced this to the Queen who rose from her throne and disappeared into St Edward's chapel.

The Dean notes an entry in the Queen's journal for 28 June 1838: "She is anything but complimentary to Archbishop Howley, who 'as usual was so confused, and puzzled and knew nothing'. This may account for the fact that 'the Archbishop most awkwardly put the ring on the wrong finger and I had the greatest difficulty to take it off again, which I did at last with great pain.' No wonder the unhappy prelate is reported to remark when all was over: 'I think we ought to have had a rehearsal.'"

By time of Victoria's great-great-granddaughter's Coronation in 1953, there were rehearsals galore. As the world's first televised Coronation ceremony, there was no room for blunders. The publishers' beautiful Coronation editions had safely gone to press long in advance, in anticipation of healthy copy sales on the big day.

The Queen and the Duke of Edinburgh.

Opposite: The Queen and The Duke of Edinburgh in ILN's 1953 Coronation issue; Women at the Royal School of Needlework embroidering the Coronation Gown; The Queen showcases the Coronation Gown, the work of Norman Hartnell

This page: Coronation covers 1953; Illustrators and writers at work in the ILN editorial office

THE KING THAT WAS AIRBRUSHED OUT OF HISTORY

Lisa Barnard, ILN's Chief Executive, reports on the
Coronation Issue that never was

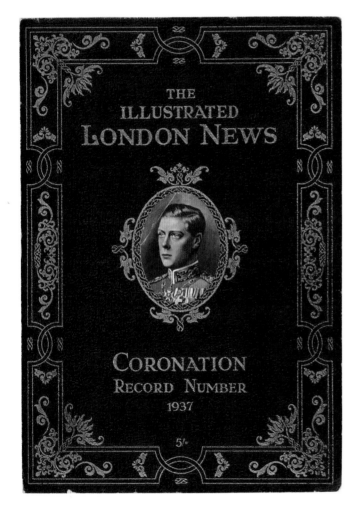

THE
ILLUSTRATED
LONDON NEWS

CORONATION
RECORD NUMBER
1937

5/-

This page: The
printer's proof of
the Coronation issue
prepared for Edward
VIII which was never
published

Unearthed in the ILN archives a few years ago was the lost edition of the Coronation Issue for King Edward VIII, a project with which the uncrowned king had cooperated in advance of his planned Coronation on 12 May 1937. Events came to pass, and it was never published.

The Illustrated London News was always privileged in its unique access to royalty, and able to commission exclusive portraits by well-known artists for special issues in advance of significant events such as Coronations and Royal Weddings.

This unpublished issue, the only one known to be in existence, contains actual portraits of Edward VIII posing in his coronation robes for celebrated artists of the period, including Fortunino Matania and Albert H Collings, as well as paintings of his crowning and homage at Westminster Abbey. Like all Coronation issues, it was prepared secretly in advance as a printer's proof, ready for publication immediately after the Coronation, and contains a few blank pages for the first photographs from the ceremony itself and for final advertisements.

There is also a handwritten note attached inside the front cover, dated 3 December 1936, by the editor, Sir Bruce Ingram, entitled "Revisions if Ed. VIII abdicates". This sets out the alterations which would need to be made to the publication, in the event of Edward VIII's abdication and the creation of a new line of succession. One week later the abdication was indeed announced, and on that day Princess Elizabeth's life changed irrevocably.

With everything ready to go to press, the abdication must have been an editor's nightmare. However, Ingrams was resourceful and immediately instructed the commissioned artist Albert H Collings to "alter" his portrait of Edward VIII and superimpose the face of his replacement, King George VI. Collings duly recycled the image, in an early version of the "airbrushing" that glossy magazines are famous for today.

The portrait was not the only item from the unpublished Edward VIII Coronation edition to be recycled. The editor was able to reuse some of the more general articles for the George VI coronation issue, and some other pictures of the coronation robes were also "altered" to show George VI - again, the artist just changed the heads. Not only was the Duke of York forced to replace his brother on the throne, as King George VI he never even got his own coronation portrait.

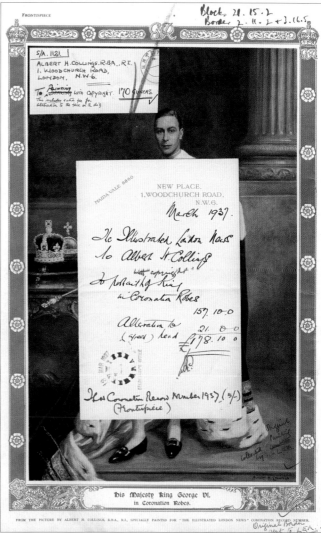

Even more resourceful, the ILN put out a special "*Abdication and Accession*" edition, including a whole essay which had been due to run in the Coronation issue. This became a tribute to Edward VIII, described as an Abdication "eulogy".

This page: (clockwise) The portrait of King Edward VIII posing in his Coronation robes, painted by Albert H Collings for the Coronation issue; The same painting replaced with the face of King George VI. The artist's bill shows he was paid a fee of £178 and 10 shillings, including £21 for the "alteration to the face"; "the crowning of King Edward VIII", that was never to be; Edward and Mrs Wallis Simpson

WHO WAS WHO

The Illustrated London News' 1953 Coronation Issue
included a roll call of "the Great and the Good".
From dukes and duchesses, ambassadors and wives,
statesmen, religious leaders, military honchos,
university chancellors to major and minor members
of the Royal Family, we feature a selection here

Sir Rupert de la Bere
LORD MAYOR OF LONDON

Mrs Henry Ford Cooper
LIBERIAN AMBASSADRESS

Cardinal Bernard Griffin
ARCHBISHOP OF WESTMINSTER

Princess Arthur Of Connaught
THE DUCHESS OF FIFE

The Rani Shanker
THE NEPALI AMBASSADRESS

Mr Augustus John
PRES. ROYAL SOC. PORTRAIT PAINTERS

The Duchess of Portland

Admiral Lord Mountbatten
COMMANDER-IN-CHIEF,
MEDITERRANEAN

His Excellency U Ka Si
BURMESE AMBASSADOR

The Duchess of Argyll

The Duke of Argyll

Dr Israel Brodie
CHIEF RABBI

Viscountess Obert de Thieusies
BELGIAN AMBASSADRESS

Dr William Neil Mckie
ORGANIST WESTMINSTER ABBEY

The Duchess of Buccleuch

Sir Donald Somervell
LORD JUSTICE OF APPEAL

Mr Gunnar Hagglof
SWEDISH
AMBASSADOR

The Duchess of Grafton

Senor Don
Domingo Derisi
ARGENTINE
AMBASSADOR

Princess Alice
COUNTESS OF
ATHLONE

Mr Roberto Mendoza
y de la Torre
CUBAN AMBASSADOR

Lord Montgomery
FIELD MARSHAL

General Sir John Crocker
ADJUTANT-GENERAL

The Duchess of Gloucester

Mr Jerzy Michalowski
POLISH AMBASSADOR

Mme Jerzy Michalowska
POLISH AMBASSADRESS

Count Eduard Reventlow
DANISH AMBASSADOR

The Duchess of Bedford

The Duchess of
Richmond and Gordon

Lord Brabazon
PRESIDENT ROYAL
INSTITUTION

The Rt. Rev. Dr C. S.
Woodward
BISHOP OF
GLOUCESTER

The Duchess of
Montrose

Mr Dudley Senayayake
PREMIER, CEYLON

The Duke of Rutland

Andrei Gromyko
SOVIET BELARUSIAN
AMBASSADOR

Sir Willoughby Norrie
GOVERNOR GENERAL
NEW ZEALAND

Gen. Sir John Harding
C.I.G.S.

Major Gwylim
Lloyd-George
MINISTER OF FOOD

The Crown Prince of
Norway

Lord Douglas of
Kirkbride
MARSHAL OF THE RAF

This page: Hosting US President John F Kennedy and his wife Jacqueline at a Buckingham Palace state banquet in 1961

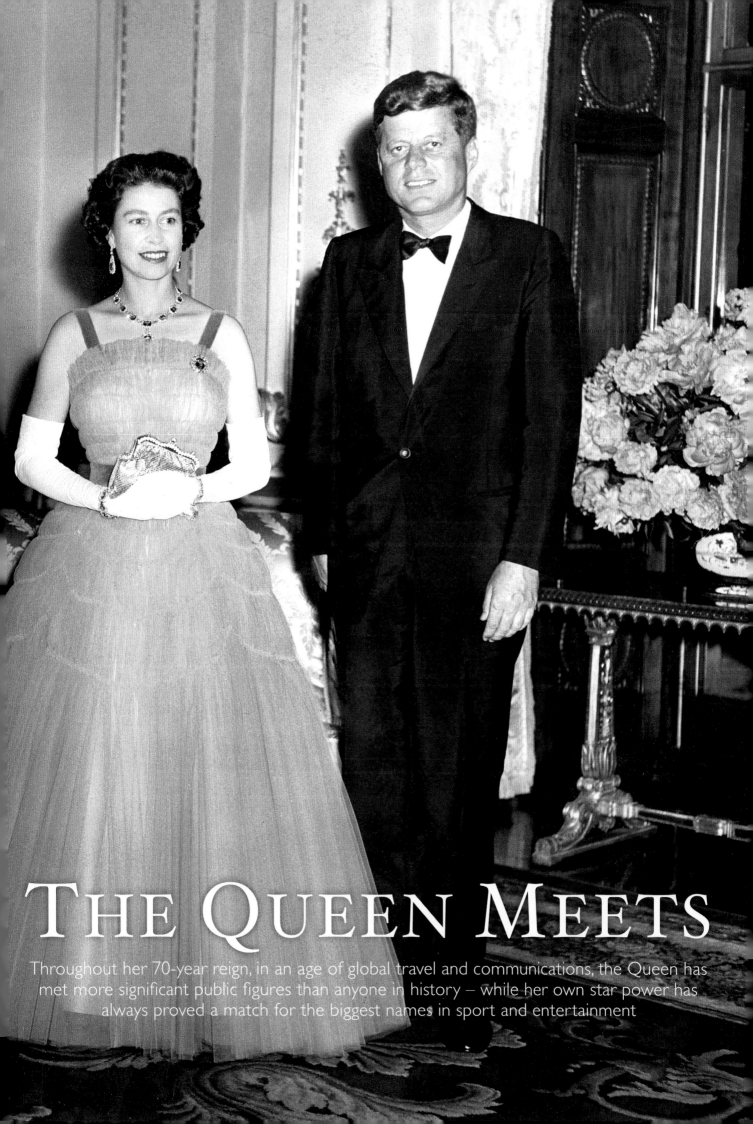

THE QUEEN MEETS

Throughout her 70-year reign, in an age of global travel and communications, the Queen has met more significant public figures than anyone in history – while her own star power has always proved a match for the biggest names in sport and entertainment

Clockwise from left:
Presenting victorious England
football captain Bobby Moore
with the World Cup, 1966;
meeting Elizabeth Taylor
in Washington, 1976; with
Michael Caine, Shirley Bassey
and Joan Collins, 1998; hosting
US President Barack Obama
and his wife Michelle, 2009;
meeting Ernie Wise and Eric
Morecambe at a film premiere,
1973; shaking hands with
Carla Bruni, wife of French
President Nicolas Sarkozy, in
2008; hosting Donald Trump
at Windsor Castle, 2018

Clockwise from top left: Receiving Canadian PM Justin Trudeau at Buckingham Palace, 2015; attending London Fashion Week with Vogue editor-in-chief Anna Wintour, 2018; out and about on the streets of London with Nelson Mandela, 1998; being introduced by Kylie Minogue to Ed Sheeran, who performed at her Diamond Jubilee Concert, 2012; much to talk about with jockey Frankie Dettori at Ascot, 2018; all smiles with Angela Merkel, 2015; looking on while Russian President Boris Yeltsin falls asleep during a Bolshoi Ballet performance, 1994; chatting with Indian Prime Minister Indira Gandhi, 1983

By Royal Warrant

A tradition that has endured for centuries, the granting of a Royal Warrant continues to evolve to serve generations of the royal family. Simon Brooke reports

When John Mills first saw an email with a login page for the Royal Warrant Holders Association, he assumed that it was some sort of hoax. Working back through his inbox, he eventually came across a previous email that explained it – his application had been successful and he was now a Royal Warrant holder to Her Majesty the Queen.

"After getting over the surprise, we were able to celebrate," he says. Mills is the President and Founder of MHR International, which provides the Royal Household with hosted HR and payroll software and reporting analytics services. The Royal Warrant certificate now hangs in his office, and the Royal Arms are proudly displayed in the company's reception. "I received so many personal emails from employees congratulating me and saying how they were also honoured to be able to say the company they work for has been granted a Royal Warrant."

To celebrate, MHR International hosted a two-day garden party at its headquarters, where employees were entertained by acrobatic performers, human tree statues and a military marching band. The finale was a spectacular aerial acrobatic display. "It was truly a special occasion, and I was delighted to share it with so many at MHR," says Mills.

Clockwise from top:
Her Majesty Queen Elizabeth II attends a banquet for the RWHA, 1967; Queen Elizabeth I used her patronage to emphasise her power; the RWHA was founded during Queen Victoria's reign; the Queen and the Duke of Edinburgh meet the staff of John Smedley, 2014

History doesn't record whether one of the very first Royal Warrant holders, Reginald de Thunderley, had a reaction to the news anything like that of MHR International. Back in 1300, de Thunderley supplied what are described as 14 striped "clothes" to be turned into uniforms for the servants of Queen Margaret, second wife of Edward I, according to historical records. Among other Warrant holders of the time were the Queen's apothecary and a fruit merchant called John.

They are separated by more than 700 years but MHR and de Thunderley are both beneficiaries of an ancient, distinguished tradition of honouring tradespeople who supply the monarch, their consort or the heir to the throne. The records of the court and the Royal Warrant Holders Association provide some fascinating historical insights.

Elizabeth I, for instance, was one of the most notable and extravagant Grantors of Royal Warrants and used her patronage, especially with her extensive wardrobe, as a way of emphasising her power and regal stature. Intriguingly, an order from one of Her Majesty's Warrant holders, a Mr George Brideman, on 28 March 1572 was for a "Night gowne" for the Earl of Leicester.

George III granted a Royal Warrant to James Swaine, his whip-maker, and James Wilkinson, the manufacturer of his guns. It was at about this time that some Grantees began to display the Royal Coats of Arms on their premises and notepaper. By 1779, Johnson and Justerini, predecessors of today's Justerini & Brooks, were proudly featuring the Prince of Wales' three-feathered badge on their letterhead, to inform the world that the company had become "Foreign Cordial Merchants" to the Prince.

By the time Queen Victoria ascended the throne there was a feeling that the use of Royal Warrants needed to be better managed and

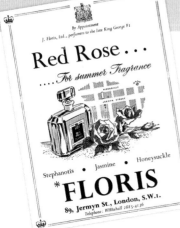

Top: John Mills and
his family with MHR's
Royal Arms
Above: The first Royal
Warrant granted to
Floris was in 1820
as comb-maker to
George IV

regulated and so, in 1840, the Royal Warrant Holders Association was founded. Today it continues to deal with applications for new Royal Warrants and amendments to more than 800 existing Warrants. It is not part of the Royal Household but works closely with the Lord Chamberlain's Office. Owned by its members, the Association not only offers advice on every aspect of being a Grantee but acts as a networking organisation through its programme of business and social events.

Royal Warrants are still very much a personal gift of the monarch. Traditionally, it was a way for the monarch to bestow patronage on tradespeople, then usually men of course, and to express gratitude for their service because it was thought that peerages and knighthoods weren't appropriate.

In a way that tradition continues. Royal Warrants are only given to suppliers of products and services, and not to those in professions such

as law and accountancy. They're also granted to a named individual within the business because historically suppliers would have been a particular tradesperson. Nowadays, this provides a useful line of responsibility for upholding the values of the Royal Warrant.

To apply for a Royal Warrant a company must have supplied one or both of the households of the two current Grantors, HM The Queen and HRH The Prince of Wales (the Duke of Edinburgh was also a Grantor until his death) for five of the past seven years. Companies need to demonstrate that they have an ongoing relationship, which is important because it emphasises consistent quality and professionalism. It also tells you something about the stability and effective management of the Grantee's business.

As part of the initial application process, which is managed by the Association, evidence of invoices and receipts is required to prove this trading relationship. A Royal Warrant is granted for up to

He called for a Djinn!

Alchemy in Alcohol No. 2

A "pink" Djinn — sorry, gin — is purely Angostura aromatic bitters and gin; nothing else! Angostura's famous aromatic flavour harmonises perfectly with gin; its subtle alchemy contriving a delightful drink popular the world over.

with

ANGOSTURA
AROMATIC BITTERS

By Appointments to Her Majesty the Queen,
Manufacturers of Angostura Aromatic Bitters.
Angostura Bitters (Dr. J. G. B. Siegert & Sons) Ltd., Port of Spain, Trinidad, B.W.I.

Left: A RWHA banquet in the 1920s
Above and below: Angostura and Justerini & Brooks are Royal Warrant holders for bitters, and wines and spirits respectively

five years, after which period the Grantee must reapply. With no guarantee that the Warrant will be continued, the Grantee needs to ensure that their goods or services are still up to scratch.

John Smedley, which produces luxury knitwear at its workshops in Derbyshire, received a Royal Warrant from the Prince of Wales on 1 April 2021, having already been granted one by the Queen in 2013.

"We liaise with key representatives of each household to ensure that we have garments available as and when required, and these are then despatched to the households. On occasions such as the Queen's visit to our Lea Mills factory in 1968, we were able to personally gift her items for her children and, in 2014, for her grandchildren," explains the company's Deputy Managing Director, Jess McGuire-Dudley. "These occasions have been very special, and our staff have all enjoyed the opportunity to present their work to the Royal Households and of course receive some royal feedback."

The Warrant application includes a sustainability questionnaire, a requirement introduced by the Prince of Wales for his Warrants back in 1990, a time when the environmental, social and governance (ESG) agenda was decidedly niche compared with today.

The requirements were extended to all Warrant holders more than 10 years ago and are defined and regulated with the help of an independent panel associated with Business in the Community, the Prince's business charity.

The Royal Warrant Holders Association has become a Friend of the Queen's Green Canopy

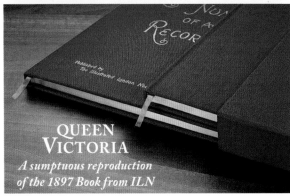

FORTNUM AND MASON

(QGC), the tree planting initiative that invites people from across the UK to "Plant a Tree for the Jubilee." The QGC will also dedicate a network of 70 ancient woodlands across the country and identify 70 ancient trees as part of the Jubilee celebrations.

In 1990, to celebrate its 150th anniversary, the Association founded The Queen Elizabeth Scholarship Trust (QEST), a charity that supports talented craftspeople through traditional college courses, vocational training, apprenticeships and one-to-one training with master artisans. Today, QEST, whose patron is the Prince of Wales, has supported more than 130 different craft disciplines, including glassmaking, willow weaving and silversmithing, and has awarded over £5million to more than 650 craftspeople.

The relationship continues with Warrant holders sponsoring budding talent and the Association partnering with events such as the recent QEST Craft Trails, when works by 12 QEST Scholars were showcased in shop windows and in stores during London Craft Week.

Although there have been suggestions that a Royal Warrant increases the value of a business by between 10 and 15 percent, Warrant holders are not permitted to trade overtly off the status. The idea is that it should be used with discretion.

"A Royal Warrant is one of the highest symbols of quality that can be bestowed on a brand," says McGuire-Dudley. "It signifies to all that our products are a certain level of craftsmanship and that's worth a great deal both internally for our staff as recognition of their great work and externally for our consumers who know we are a brand they can believe in. Whether a brand is heritage or modern, it's about quality."

She points to new initiatives introduced into the Warrant application process that are increasingly focused on sustainability. "That's an important way for us to keep our work on track, share our progress and reach a new generation of consumers where our message really hits home – 'Invest in quality products and keep them for longer.'"

"The Royal Warrant is the most coveted award in the world for acknowledging the finest products made in the UK," says Alan Cosby, Chairman and Managing Director of Kent Brushes. The company prizes a note from the then Princess Elizabeth dated 30 January 1948 offering thanks for a dressing-table set. "The Royal Arms on our products and packaging is recognised by our customers worldwide, but in particular for exports to the US, Japan, China and Korea."

Companies are allowed to use the relevant Royal Coat of Arms on products and packaging,

Above: A royal visit to Fortnum & Mason during the Diamond Jubilee, 2012
Left: Nick and Ruth Jubert, of Warrant-holder Dennys Brands, suppliers of catering clothing, with the tree they have planted for the Queen's Green Canopy

Top: The Queen talks with chef Anton Mosimann, then RWHA president, and his wife Katrin, as she renews the Association's Royal Charter, 2007

Above: A royal visit to Tate & Lyle's Liverpool factory at Huskisson Dock, 1958

stationery, marketing communications, vehicles and their premises, although not all companies can use it in all of these situations.

Where things go wrong, the Association is keen to stress, it's usually just a mistake or a misinterpretation rather than a deliberate pushing of boundaries.

Non-British companies have held Royal Warrants for many years, usually where an equivalent British supplier is not easily available. These include French Champagne houses such as Bollinger, Louis Roederer and Moët & Chandon as well as Angostura, creator of the famous bitters and based in Trinidad and Tobago.

With globalisation, the number of international groups with a Royal Warrant has expanded over the years.

Like the monarchy itself, the Association is clearly aware that the business of granting and managing Royal Warrants needs to evolve. Technology, lifestyles and tastes change and, when future Royal Warrant Grantors are selected, their choices will reflect this evolution.

Such shifts are a way of staying relevant to commerce, industry and society in the 21st century and supporting new holders and generations of the royal family, while continuing to celebrate the traditions of Royal Warrant-holding that have endured for centuries.

CROCKETT & JONES

MADE IN ENGLAND | SINCE 1879

Connaught

in Black Calf

Our best-selling Cap Oxford,
availalbe in Black, Dark Brown &
Chestnut Calf.

Classic English shoemaking at its finest.

CROCKETTANDJONES.COM

BY ROYAL APPOINTMENT

improving channel performance

Adexchange congratulates Her Majesty The Queen on her Platinum Jubilee

Adexchange is a multilingual communications agency that specialises in improving customer journeys. We deliver measurable improvement across all communication channels including FAQs, Chatbots and IVRs by streamlining content, design and touchpoint strategy.

www.adexchange.co.uk

ANGOSTURA® bitters

House of Angostura® offers its warmest congratulations to HM The Queen on the occasion of Her Majesty's Platinum Jubilee

ANGOSTURA® aromatic bitters is proud to hold a Royal Warrant of Appointment from HM Queen Elizabeth II since 1955. We wish Her Majesty good health and continued happiness

www.angosturabitters.com

APEX LIFTS

a CAPITAL success

Established in 1970, Apex Lifts provide a multitude of lift services, from maintenance to modernisation. Honoured to have held a Royal Warrant to HM The Queen for many years, we congratulate Her Majesty on the celebration of her Platinum Jubilee.

www.apexlifts.com

Bendicks congratulates Her Majesty The Queen on the occasion of her Platinum Jubilee

For over 90 years Bendicks has created fine chocolates, including the world-famous Bendicks Bittermint. As proud holders of the Royal Warrant for 60 years, the company is dedicated to producing the finest mint chocolates and has established an unrivalled reputation for quality, making Bendicks the perfect choice for all dinner and entertaining occasions.

www.bendicks.co.uk

C&I Controls would like to congratulate HM The Queen on the occasion of Her Majesty's Platinum Jubilee

C&I Controls established in 1989, focusing on high-quality workmanship, service and delivery. We provide bespoke electrical mechanical design and installation services, for industrial and commercial properties. Working with market-leading manufacturers so that our customers are assured of the highest standards at all times.

cicontrols@cicontrols.co.uk

COVENTRY SCAFFOLDING

LONDON EST 1950

Coventry Scaffolding sends its very best wishes to Her Majesty The Queen on her Platinum Jubilee

Coventry Scaffolding has enjoyed over 70 years of success as one of London's largest independent scaffolders. We are proud to have been able to serve the Royal Household for over 40 years. An achievement which has earned us the privilege of working on some of the nation's most prestigious buildings.

www.coventry.scaffolding.com

These pages contain messages from a selection of members
of The Royal Warrant Holders Association, congratulating
Her Majesty Queen Elizabeth II on the occasion of her Platinum Jubilee

Congratulations to Her Majesty The Queen on the momentous occasion of her Platinum Jubilee

Since 1879, Crockett & Jones has been producing some of the finest footwear in the world from its factory in Northampton, the shoemaking capital of England. The business is still owned and managed by the founding family, who emphasise quality and timeless style above all else.

www.crockettandjones.co.uk

From one Crown to another, congratulations on your Platinum Jubilee

At Crown, we have always admired those who proudly put their personal mark on things. For most that means brightening up a home, but for others it's about brightening a nation. Thank you for 70 brilliant years.

www.crownpaints.co.uk

DAKS would like to congratulate Her Majesty The Queen on the occasion of her Platinum Jubilee

DAKS

DAKS, the quintessentially British brand established in 1894, offers fine tailoring for men and women. We are proud to have held Her Majesty's Royal Warrant as outfitters since 1962. Our staff and associates are humbly honoured to express their warmest and loyal congratulations to Her Majesty on her Platinum Jubilee.

www.daks.com

FLORIS
LONDON

As the Appointed Perfumers to Her Majesty The Queen, and on behalf of all the Floris family and staff, it is our great pleasure to extend our warmest congratulations to Her Majesty The Queen on this remarkable milestone of her Platinum Jubilee.

www.florislondon.com

GILKES

Gilkes would like to congratulate Her Majesty on the occasion of her Platinum Jubilee

We are delighted to have had the honour of serving Queen Elizabeth II during her 70-year reign. Gilkes is an international manufacturing company based in Cumbria. Gilkes designs, manufactures and supplies hydroelectric turbines and ancillary equipment.

www.gilkes.com

HAMILTON & INCHES
ESTABLISHED 1866

Hamilton & Inches sends Her Majesty The Queen best wishes on the occasion of her Platinum Jubilee

Hamilton & Inches is honoured to have held a Royal Warrant for over 120 years as silversmiths and clock specialists to Her Majesty The Queen. These skills remain at the core of Hamilton & Inches, fostering unique crafts and artisans in its workshops of silversmiths, goldsmiths, watchmakers and hand-engravers.

www.hamiltonandinches.com

HAND & LOCK
- SINCE 1767 -

Hand & Lock would like to congratulate Her Majesty The Queen on the very special occasion of Her Majesty's Platinum Jubilee

We have celebrated each milestone with the British Monarch through embroidery since 1767 and are proud to be part of this historic moment. For further information please contact Jessica Pile on + 44 020 7580 7488

www.handembroidery.com

HEIRLOOMS
ENGLAND

Warmest congratulations to Her Majesty The Queen on the historic occasion of her Platinum Jubilee

Established in 1984 to manufacture luxury linens, Heirlooms is honoured to be By Appointment to Her Majesty The Queen and His Royal Highness The Prince of Wales.

www.heirlooms-linens.com

QEST
The Royal Warrant Holders Association
Queen Elizabeth Scholarship Trust
CHARITY

SUPPORTING
EXCELLENCE
IN BRITISH
CRAFTSMANSHIP

CRAFTING A LOVING LEGACY

The patronage of the Royal Albert Hall by two unique partnerships will be celebrated with four brand-new life-sized sculptures by talented artisans very close to home. Charlotte McManus reports

O n 29 March 1871, Queen Victoria marked a significant new chapter in British culture with the opening of the Royal Albert Hall. Conceived by, and named after, the Queen's late husband, Prince Albert, the splendid South Kensington building encapsulated the spirit of royal patronage as well as the couple's lifelong commitment to the arts.

Above: Royal Warrant holder John Lobb lent Field an Oxford shoe for reference in sculpting Prince Philip's outfit
Opposite: Field's maquette armatures made of wood, welded steel, aluminium wire and a table leg

150 years on, the Hall, now one of the UK's most celebrated venues, is commemorating its landmark anniversary with four new life-sized sculptures inspired by royal patrons past and present. This landmark commission has given talented young British artisans the chance to create works that will go on permanent display upon their reveal in summer 2022.

When it came to choosing talent to commission for this once-in-a-lifetime project, only one organisation was considered – QEST (the Queen Elizabeth Scholarship Trust), a charity that supports excellence in British craftsmanship and the vital education of gifted artisans.

"We have a long relationship with the Royal Warrant Holders Association (of which QEST is a charity), and we share an aspiration to support British craftsmanship," says Louise Halliday, Director of External Affairs at the Hall. "The sculptures will fill the North Porch and South Porch niches with figures that represent the Hall's history – and Prince Albert's original aspiration for a Hall for the arts and sciences for everyone."

Having lain empty since 1871, the niche in the North Porch, the Hall's original royal entrance, will be filled by sculptures of Queen Victoria and Prince Albert, while the South Porch,

constructed in 2003, will feature bespoke sculptures of Her Majesty the Queen, the Hall's current patron, and her husband, the late Duke of Edinburgh.

As QEST launched a dedicated design competition among its alumni, shortlisted entrants were judged against rigorous criteria, from design approach and practicality to suitability for both the subjects and locations. After all, creating sculptures for an institution as venerable as the Grade I-listed Royal Albert Hall comes with a whole host of complex factors, not least planning permission.

"The sculptors had to consider the Hall's heritage and conservation," says Halliday. "The materials used were a major consideration in terms of appropriateness, colour, durability, cost and even weight."

After much deliberation, the two winners were confirmed in November 2021.

Poppy Field scooped the assignment for the South Porch sculptures. Specialising in bronze figurative sculpture, Field was elated to receive her first ever public commission.

"I was as surprised as I was euphoric," she says. "I felt so fortunate that the committee had entrusted me with this responsibility."

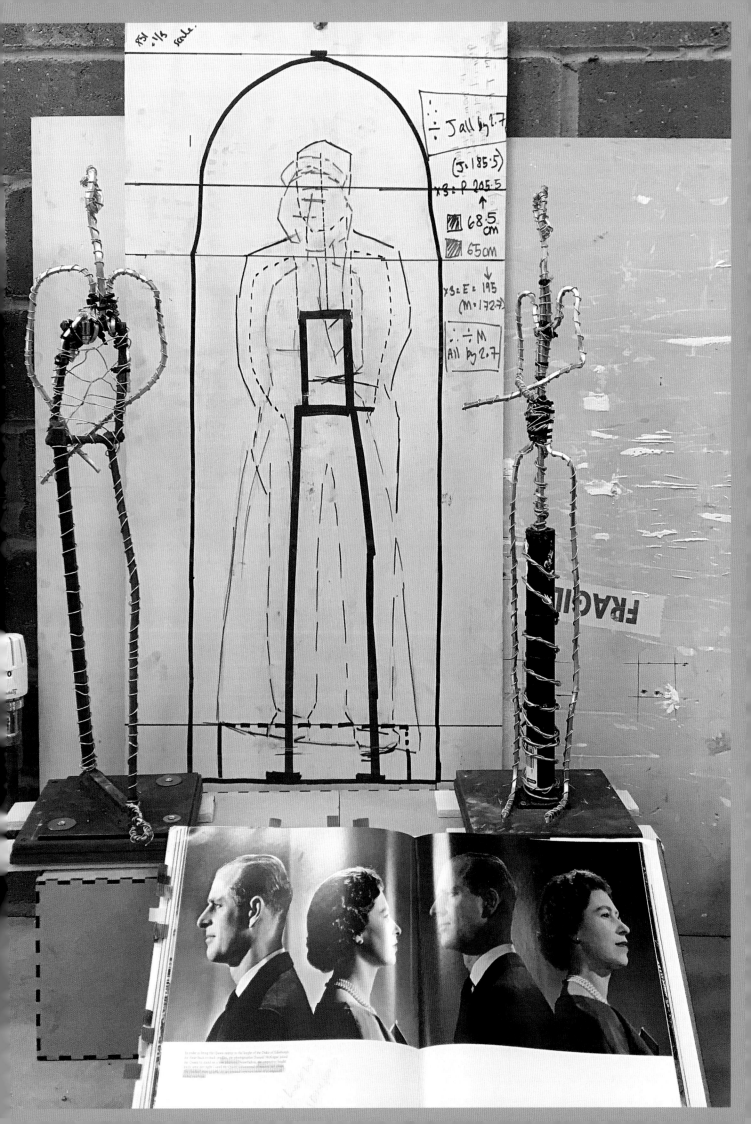

Field's interpretation of the South Porch competition brief – which simply called for 'a contemporary treatment' that recognised Her Majesty as 'our modern patron' – was to "explore a connection between the Royal Albert Hall as 'The Nation's Village Hall' and The Queen and Prince Philip's relationship with the public".

Field describes how viewers will follow Prince Philip's gaze from his position on the left niche over to the figure of the Queen on the right. "Viewers will see the Queen's sculpture set at an angle, as if she were about to turn into the Hall, and, if involved with this psychological narrative, turn their attention to the doorway and feel 'welcomed' into the Hall."

Complementing the Hall's distinctive brickwork, the sculptures will be cast in bronze with a deep brown patina and ferric red undertones. Various royal regalia will decorate the couple, including The Most Noble Order of the Garter. The sculpture of Her Majesty will also feature representations of the Vladimir Tiara with its distinctive hanging emeralds, and the Edinburgh Wedding Bracelet, given to the Queen by Prince Philip on the day of their nuptials.

Field's vision was fuelled by intensive research. Books, photographs and footage of the royals were consumed in droves, while reaching out to those with personal royal connections proved invaluable in determining appropriate age and dress. Royal Warrant Holders also pitched in, with tailor Gieves & Hawkes and bootmaker John Lobb lending styles to use as design references. Glovemaker Cornelia James contributed a bespoke accessory to model from.

Designing the North Porch is London Stone Carving, a craft collective based in London. QEST Scholars Tom Nicholls and Tom Brown were awarded the commission alongside their colleagues Josh Locksmith and Sam Lee – their sculptures are very much a group effort.

The quartet began by creating wax maquettes of Victoria and Albert before living models dressed in replica clothing were used to shape life-sized clay figures, from which detailed moulds were made.

Each North Porch sculpture is hewn from two hefty blocks of statuary-grade Portland stone, every element carved by hand. Garbed in draped robes and regal insignia, the forms of Queen Victoria and Prince Albert will be crafted in intricately rich detail.

Opposite: Jesmonite casts used in the planning permission application
This page: The statues of Victoria and Albert were hewn from two blocks of statuary-grade Portland Stone, after first creating wax maquettes

"We sculpted the pair in classical style, but gave them a subtly contemporary attitude," say the London Stone Carving team. "Albert and Victoria are depicted on the eve of 1851's Great Exhibition, an event which raised the funds to construct the Royal Albert Hall and The V&A – both now iconic pieces of our cultural heritage. Our sculptures represent the royals in their youth, showing mutual affection in their understated gesturing toward one another while simultaneously welcoming visitors approaching the Hall from Hyde Park."

Though the past months have been something of a whirlwind in getting the sculptures ready for display, their creators are eagerly anticipating how their works might be received by the public.

"We would like people to see a warmth expressed by the royal couple that may not have been depicted before, to feel that the works are so comfortable in the Hall's magnificent facade that visitors might wonder if the sculptures are new, or have always been there," says London Stone Carving.

"I have striven to imbue my sculptures with something universal and relatable," adds Field. "After all, the partnership of Her Majesty the Queen and Prince Philip might just be one of the greatest stories of our time."

QEST

QEST, the Queen Elizabeth Scholarship Trust, was founded in 1990, when Queen Elizabeth The Queen Mother graciously agreed that a new charity formed by the Royal Warrant Holders Association, then in its 150th year, could bear her name. QEST's mission is to support excellence in British craftsmanship, from investing in talent and funding education to helping to preserve craft skills for future generations. Having awarded over £5m to more than 650 makers so far, many of the nation's most exceptional craftspeople have benefited from QEST support. For every copy of this Platinum Jubilee publication sold, 50p will be donated to QEST. For more information, or to get involved with QEST, visit qest.org.uk

A FAMILY AFFAIR

Despite her exalted status, the Queen has long shared the challenge of working mothers everywhere – balancing the obligations of her role with the ups and downs of family life

BLISSFUL CHILDHOOD

If there is one foundation stone that sets the Queen apart from many of her forebears on the British throne, it is the loving and nurturing environment in which she grew up. As her mother once remarked to a dinner companion, "As a family, we enjoy things so."

Blessed with a calm, harmonious family life, at least until the abdication, Princess Elizabeth was close to both her parents but especially fond of her father, and happy to be his constant companion in shooting, walking and riding. In return, he referred to his elder daughter as "my pride" and shared with her his devotion to duty, a quality that would be a priceless asset in her future role.

SISTER ACT

The Queen's younger sister, Princess Margaret Rose, was one of the very few people to have always spoken her mind in front of the monarch. While the pair were inseparable as youngsters, in adult life they did very much their own thing – Elizabeth busy on regal duties, Margaret occupying herself with more artistic and cultural diversions. Unhappy for a while after her broken romance with Captain Peter Townsend, the Princess went on to marry Antony Armstrong-Jones and have two children. Following her divorce in 1978, Margaret courted controversy – from her lavish holidays on Mustique to her relationship with the much younger Roddy Llewellyn. But throughout her personal trials and public scandals, Margaret's relationship with the Queen endured and towards the end of her life, she spoke with her sister on the phone almost every day. The Queen appreciated that Margaret understood her and her unique life like no-one else.

Clockwise from left: The princesses performing Cinderella, 1942; a piano duet, 1940; matched in satin for Margaret's 50th birthday, 1980; a family day out, 1935; the sisters sit for an ILN centenary portrait, 1942

A LIFELONG PARTNERSHIP

Another great stroke of fortune for Princess Elizabeth was meeting the young Lieutenant Philip Mountbatten, and deciding that he, and no other, would be her husband. The years that followed their wedding in 1947 were among the most carefree the Queen has ever known, including time in Malta where she got to lead the normal life of a navy wife. Philip, who was made HRH The Duke of Edinburgh on his wedding day, was the person who broke it to Elizabeth that she had become Queen, he was by her side when she was crowned, and there he remained through an astonishing 73 years of marriage. While he settled for the role of Consort, always one step behind his wife in public, his strong personality shone through and it was quite clearly a partnership of equals through all the triumphs and tribulations of any long union. On their Golden Wedding anniversary, the Queen toasted her husband as "quite simply, my strength and stay all these years".

**Opposite page,
clockwise from top left:**
A handwritten thank you
letter from the Queen,
1960; on the way to Royal
Ascot in Windsor Great
Park, 2014; the marriage
licence and certificate of
the royal couple, 1947; on
honeymoon at Broadlands
This page: "Quite simply,
my strength and stay"

THE QUEEN'S CHILDREN

Princess Elizabeth became a young mother just as her role as heir presumptive meant her life became extraordinarily busy. With two children under five at the time of her Coronation, the Queen and Duke of Edinburgh often spent long periods away from Prince Charles and Princess Anne, something that was less strange at the time than it is now. As the Duke of Edinburgh later reflected on their abilities as parents, "We did our best."

By the time her two younger sons came along nearly a decade later, the Queen had relaxed into her role and was able to spend more time with her children. However, her challenges as a mother continued into her middle age. Both she and the Duke could only observe from the sidelines as three of their four children went through messy separations and divorce played out in front of the world's media. The Queen has always done her best to keep 'the Firm' on an even keel but even she admitted in 1992 that her family problems, plus a terrible fire at Windsor Castle, had caused her to reflect on her "annus horribilis".

While Prince Charles has long prepared for his future role as King, other members of the royal family have also stepped to the fore. Prince Edward's wife, the Countess of Wessex, has grown increasingly close to Her Majesty, while Princess Anne has for many years carried out the highest number of public engagements. She has clearly inherited the work ethic of her mother, just as Princess Elizabeth did from her parents.

Top: The royal family filmed having lunch for an ITV documentary, 1969
Above: The Queen and Prince Philip with their four children at Windsor, 1968

TRUEFITT&HILL

EST. 1805 · ST. JAMES'S · LONDON

GROOMING MEN FOR GREATNESS SINCE 1805

In every age, for all generations, Truefitt & Hill is an invaluable asset to all well groomed men.
From our personalised barbershop services to our finely crafted products, we provide the guidance,
confidence, knowledge, tools and inspiration every man needs to put his best face forward.

www.truefittandhill.co.uk

Image shot at St. James's Hotel & Club Mayfair

Clockwise from top: Princes William and Harry have grown up under the spotlight; Princesses Eugenie and Beatrice at William's wedding, 2011; Zara Tindall has followed in the family riding tradition; Lady Louise Windsor at the Royal Windsor Horse Show, 2021

THE QUEEN'S GRANDCHILDREN

The Queen has eight grandchildren in total. While Princes William and Harry have always received a huge amount of public attention, the challenge for every branch of this generation is to balance modern family life and meaningful career while supporting the traditional values of the monarchy.

Princess Anne's daughter Zara Tindall has been the most recognisable chip off the old block, inheriting her grandparents' and parents' love of horse riding, and competing all the way to the Olympics.

Princesses Beatrice and Eugenie have weathered the storms of their parents' divorce and ensuing controversies, carving out professional roles for themselves and starting their own families.

Of particular delight to the Queen, the teenage Lady Louise Windsor has acquired a passion for carriage-driving, a sport she enjoyed learning from her grandfather. After the Duke of Edinburgh's death in 2021, Lady Louise paid a touching tribute by driving his carriage at the Royal Windsor Horse Show.

In September 2021, Princess Beatrice gave birth to Sienna Elizabeth, Her Majesty's 12th grandchild. Her heir the Prince of Wales may be focused on slimming down the public face of monarchy but, on the personal side at least, the Queen's family is proving an ever-expanding brood.

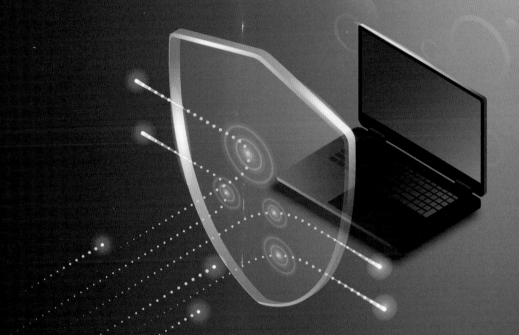

MA'AM
WEARS IT WELL

For nearly a century, the Queen has confounded changing fashions and trends to enjoy
her own sense of style, perfectly suited to every occasion

Above: The Queen in Norman Hartnell, photographed by Cecil Beaton **Opposite:** To stand out in a crowd, the Queen has a wardrobe full of bright colours

The most photographed woman in the world, the Queen has a look that is all her own. Over the course of nearly a century, while never becoming a fashion icon like so many other royal figures, she has instead carved out a style that has never succumbed to the changing trends, but has seamlessly evolved alongside them. Whether she is at her most regal with her courtly gowns set against the splendid backdrop of British castles and overseas palaces, or at her most relaxed in comfy tweeds and a cardigan, the Queen always dresses unmistakably like the Queen. In an era when every public figure's look is endlessly scrutinised and imitated, that is no small thing.

The Queen, an intensely practical woman, has always seen her wardrobe as one more aspect of the job she was born to perform. For example, it is no coincidence that her outfits on public occasions have so often been composed of bright blocks of colour. She says herself, "I have to be seen to be believed," and dressing in rich red or bright pastel blue ensures she can be spotted easily in large crowds. The Queen realises she has a unique job and her clothes must be fit for purpose. If the colours are strong, the tailoring is smart, understated and discreet. Her outfits must be as comfortable and hard-wearing as possible, with skirts often stitched with small weights inside the hems to guard against windy weather, and lengths never immodest. Her hat brims must be big enough to be distinctive, but not so big that they hide her face or create problems getting in and out of cars. Dressing the Queen is a delightful challenge of marrying elegance with practicality, and it is one that has evolved naturally for her stylists and dressmakers over many years.

Throughout her childhood, the young Princess Elizabeth was dressed neatly but unimaginatively, often in an outfit to match that of her younger sister Margaret. While she was never less than picture-perfect, the Princess's lack of interest in clothes was noticed by her governess, Marion Crawford, who wrote later how her young charge "was always conservative in her dress and content to wear whatever was laid out for her". Even when the talents of courtly couturier Norman Hartnell were called upon to design the Princess's very first party dress after the war, he commented on how "she accepted her fittings as part of her official duties, but one did not feel she was interested in clothes or even following the latest fashions".

This indifference continued into her young adulthood, much to the dismay of fashion commentators, who noticed the clear sartorial influence of Queen Elizabeth in her elder daughter's choices of draped bodices, muted colours and softly curved hats. While she was universally considered a beautiful young woman, her clothes were not those of a chic, fashion-forward young princess that so many had hoped for.

THE TATLER AND BYSTANDER

NOV. 5
1952

THE QUEEN LEAVES AFTER
A ROYAL ENTERTAINMENT

NORMAN HARTNELL

No fashion designer can claim a closer association with the Queen than Norman Hartnell. After he became her first couturier with a bridesmaid dress for the wedding of Princess Alice, Duchess of Gloucester in 1935, Elizabeth turned to him on the two biggest days of her life. For her wedding to Philip Mountbatten in 1947, he created her Botticelli-inspired gown, embroidered with 10,000 seed pearls and thousands of white beads, and then six years later came his masterpiece. The Queen's coronation gown, chosen from one of nine sketched designs he initially submitted, was hand-embroidered with flower symbols of the United Kingdom and its dominions. Expert cutters and fitters were required to support the work of Hartnell, who couldn't actually sew himself, despite being a master of construction and fabric. As well as the Queen's gown that day, Hartnell designed the dresses for her maids of honour, as well as for all the other leading royal ladies inside Westminster Abbey. The designer continued to work for the Queen until shortly before his death in 1979 and she wore outfits from the House of Hartnell into the 1980s.

Left to right:
A Tudor-inspired hat to match Norman Hartnell's primrose coat for Prince Charles's investiture as Prince of Wales, 1969; wearing Hartnell's much-copied 'Magpie' dress to the Royal Film Performance in 1952; an illustration of Hartnell's coronation gown

Early in her reign, however, her sense of style began to evolve. The 1940s trend of a New Look silhouette suited her well, emphasising her neat figure and tiny waist. The regal splendour of her coronation paved the way for a young Queen who appeared to enjoy wearing a succession of dazzling evening gowns either by Norman Hartnell or Hardy Amies, and adding any combination of dazzling gems from her unique collection, jewels she wore with a becoming insouciance which, paired with her fresh-faced appeal, only added to the glamour.

A picture of the young Queen dressed for an evening engagement on the arm of a dinner-suited Duke of Edinburgh made a strong impression, and copies of her outfits began to fly off the shelves. Hartnell's famous 'Magpie' dress for the Queen at the Royal Command Film Performance in 1952, a simple but striking black gown with a slash of white at the front, saw versions on sale in shops within days. Hartnell began to go to great lengths to keep his designs secret, and to make them more complicated to avoid being copied.

Throughout the decades of her reign, the Queen has always seemed perfectly happy for other royal women to occupy the covers of fashion magazines. Even so, it is clear she has her favourite designers who have remained on call for the big events in Her Majesty's diary, and these creative talents have just as complex a brief as any working for the Princess of Wales in the 1980s and 1990s or, more recently, the Duchess of Cambridge.

For more than a decade, Stewart Parvin has been a regular go-to for the Queen and other members of the royal family, including getting the commission for Zara Tindall's wedding dress. It was Parvin who was set to work for President Obama's state visit in 2011, and he has no doubt who really sets the creative tone for each outfit. In an interview, he once explained that the Queen knows "exactly what she wants" when it comes to her clothes. "They have to be beautifully made. The quality of them is as important as the style. The Queen can't wear the same outfit as anyone else."

The Queen's most invaluable style consultant these days is Angela Kelly, her senior dresser since 2002. In recognition of her close rapport with her employer, Kelly has more recently been promoted to Curator to Her Majesty the Queen (Jewellery, Insignia and Wardrobe). As well as advising on choice of outfit for all and every occasion, Kelly books fittings and offers up her own designs – she created the primrose yellow suit worn by the Queen for the wedding of the Duke and Duchess of Cambridge in 2011.

Under Kelly's supervision, the Queen's dressers care for all her clothes, as well as keeping records of her ever-expanding wardrobe, including when and where each item has had an outing. While every royal outfit must be suited to a particular occasion, the Queen's hundreds of trips abroad have offered the

HARDY AMIES

Hardy Amies' work first came to the attention of Princess Elizabeth in 1950, when she admired the clothes of her lady-in-waiting Lady Alice Egerton, soon summoned their designer to Clarence House and asked him to contribute to her wardrobe for a forthcoming tour of Canada. Within five years, Amies had been appointed one of the Queen's three official dressmakers with a Royal Warrant to his name, and was significant in moulding her new, crisp, understated style of dress. Throughout the 1960s and 1970s, Amies steered the Queen carefully through sharper, more modern silhouettes, although he did once bemoan the rising hemline of the 1960s, complaining it made it very challenging to dress the Queen with dignity. In 1990, in an interview with The Illustrated London News, Amies revealed that the Queen grumbled about his prices, a revelation that cannot have gone down too well at the Palace, although it does demonstrate the dilemma of the monarch, like many a royal, of wanting to dress the part without appearing needlessly extravagant.

HATS OFF

It is extremely rare that the Queen is seen on a public engagement, particularly one that takes her anywhere outside, without a hat. She grew up in an age when all well-dressed ladies were expected to cover their heads and, to this day, she appears to look slightly incomplete without one. Her choice of hat is a key element of the Queen's individual style and sometimes allows her to express herself in a way that her outfit cannot.

Her first hat designers were Kate Day and Danish-born Aage Thaarup, an established milliner favoured by her mother, and who worked with Hartnell to match clothes to headwear. Perhaps Thaarup's most famous creation was the felt beret with ostrich feather pom-poms the Queen wore with her love-in-the-mist blue going-away outfit by Hartnell. He also designed the distinctive bearskin tricorn worn by the Queen at Trooping the Colour.

Simone Mirman created numerous hats for the Queen including many feminine, floral headpieces which were to characterise her formal headwear of the 1960s, before Hardy Amies began to work with the Australian milliner Freddie Fox in 1968. By the time of his retirement in 2002, Fox had created 350 hats for the Queen, including the unusual pink hat with fabric flowers she wore during her City of London walkabout for the Silver Jubilee in 1977.

More recently, it was Philip Somerville who created most of the Queen's hats, and could claim much credit for her distinctive shift to broader-brimmed styles. Since 2014, Rachel Trevor-Morgan has held a Royal Warrant for the Queen's headwear, and there can be no busier milliner than the one working for our monarch.

opportunity to make an especially symbolic gesture to her hosts through her choice of clothing and accessories. At a state dinner in Lahore in 1961, she deliberately wore a gown by Hartnell in white and green – Pakistan's national colours – while in 1983 during a visit to California, she charmed her hosts with an evening dress designed by Amies, covered in beaded poppies.

Even in more informal surroundings, the Queen is able to express herself through her clothes, often adding a particularly significant piece of jewellery to an otherwise unremarkable outfit. A brooch from the royal collection can tell a powerful story!

If for every occasion her clothes are a practical extension of what the Queen considers her unique job, never is this more in evidence than when she is off duty. Throughout her reign, come fair weather or foul, her subjects have been reassured by pictures of the monarch setting out in her country 'uniform' – flat shoes or boots, warm woollen skirt (very occasionally trousers), a weatherproof mackintosh, Barbour jacket or Burberry coat and, invariably, the silk headscarf. It may not be typical courtly glamour, but as with all her outfits, the Queen has made this look one that is forever associated with her own brand of majesty.

Clockwise: Poppies for California; in pink and green by Hardy Amies; blue chiffon for Charles and Diana's wedding, together with original sketch by designer Ian Thomas; Norman Hartnell's green and white dress for Pakistan

THE
QUEEN
AND HER
FOUR-
LEGGED
FRIENDS

Throughout her life, the Queen has always enjoyed the company of horses, while her dogs, including her beloved corgis, have never been far away

In 2014, celebrated war surgeon David Nott was invited to Buckingham Palace for lunch and found himself seated next to the Queen. When she asked him about his recent traumatic experiences overseas, he found himself overcome and unable to speak. Quick to realise his plight, Her Majesty beckoned a courtier to let in her corgis, who immediately went underneath the table. The Queen opened a nearby biscuit tin, turned to Nott and suggested, "Why don't we feed the dogs?" And for the next 20 minutes, that's exactly what they did.

During the Queen's long and eventful life, through times both happy and more challenging, one constant has been her canine companions – most famously the corgis that have long been associated with Her Majesty, but also labradors and spaniels.

The Queen is by no means the first dog lover in her family. Her father George VI was also often accompanied by a labrador, while her uncle the Duke of Windsor had a fondness for cairn terriers and later a penchant for pugs. Their father George V's favourite was clumber spaniels, and before that Queen Victoria and Queen Alexandra owned hundreds of dogs between them.

For the Queen as for her predecessors, her dogs provide affection, loyalty and, something she no doubt values highly, complete discretion. In the midst of her extraordinary life, they also provide a welcome dose of normality. A world away from her ceremonial duties, she keeps them close to her at home and likes to mix their meals herself. They go where she goes and, among the hundreds of photographs of her relaxing at her various residences, there is seldom a snap without at least a couple of dogs in the frame.

Left: For the Queen, dogs have always been an essential part of the family

Above: Princess Elizabeth with one of the horses during harvest at Sandringham, 1943

Her love of horses has proved just as enduring, with photographs of young Princess Elizabeth on a tiny pony making way for the young Queen in full gallop at Ascot. More recently, she has been regularly spotted trekking in Windsor Great Park, come rain or shine, well into her 10th decade.

While the Duke of Edinburgh was the more celebrated carriage driver, the Queen won her own medal in this sport at the Royal Windsor Horse Show of 1944. She was also coached in riding side-saddle from a young age, a skill she long deployed while reviewing troops. She rode publicly at Trooping the Colour until 1986, only stopping when her favourite parade horse Burmese retired. At the 1981 ceremony when six blank shots were fired causing panic in the crowd, the Queen remained steady on her mount, pausing to reassure her horse before riding on.

This confidence in the saddle is something she has passed on to her family members, with both her daughter Princess Anne and granddaughter Zara Phillips riding competitively, going on to compete in equestrian events at the Olympic Games of 1976 and 2012 respectively. At the London Games, Zara was cheered on by other family members as she earned her country a silver medal.

The Queen's passion for racing is clear, with the sight of her perched on a Land Rover, binoculars pinned to her face, a regular occurrence at riding events around the country. And as a respected and highly knowledgeable owner, she never looks happier than when one of her horses comes in first past the post at Ascot.

When she was still very young, the Queen told her riding instructor Horace Smith that, had she not been who she was, she would "like to be a lady living in the country with lots of horses and dogs". It would seem that, despite her unique status, she has gone a long way to achieving this.

THE QUEEN'S BEST FRIENDS – HER CORGIS

The young Princess Elizabeth was just seven years old when she first met a corgi belonging to the family of the Marquess of Bath, and returned home speaking of little else. Her parents already owned labradors and a Japanese lion dog called Choo-choo, but she soon persuaded them to add another to their pack, and Pembrokeshire corgi Dookie duly arrived. The Duke of York fondly called him "the black sheep of the family" and he was cheeky, spoiled and unconditionally adored. Dookie became the first of many dogs, adding to an atmosphere of happy domesticity whenever the royal family were pictured.

Elizabeth received her first own corgi, Susan, for her 18th birthday, and the pair proved so inseparable that the dog accompanied the Princess on her honeymoon in 1947. When she was buried at Sandringham in 1959, her gravestone was marked, "For 15 years the Queen's faithful companion." It is from Susan that the royal corgi dynasty is descended, with the Queen reported to have owned up to 30 dogs in her lifetime – all lucky hounds who have enjoyed the most luxurious of canine existences,

with menus served up by a gourmet chef and Christmas stockings prepared by the Queen herself. As well as corgis, there has been the odd 'dorgi', following an unplanned union between Elizabeth's corgi Tiny and Princess Margaret's daschund, Pipkin. While the Queen gave up breeding in 2015, the sound of paws is still heard throughout the royal residences. In June 2021, on what would have been the Duke of Edinburgh's 100th birthday, she was given a corgi puppy by her family, clearly recognising she would have enjoyed no better comfort.

Left: Young Elizabeth gives her corgi a hug, 1936
Above: When the royals go to different homes, pets go too. Windsor Castle, 1959

THE UK'S No.1 WHISKY

We'll be raising a glass to
congratulate Her Majesty The Queen
on her Platinum Jubilee celebrations.
Here's to a Famous year.

THE FAMOUS GROUSE

Source: Nielsen, Total Trade, w/ending 01.01.22

thefamousgrouse.com

A STABLE OF WINNERS

Staff at every royal residence know there is one publication the Queen must not be without of a morning. Ahead of all the newspapers with their headlines, she will invariably seek out the Racing Post.

Besides her own lifelong affinity with horses and love of riding since she was given her first Shetland pony aged four, the Queen's most serious and enduring pastime away from ceremonial duties is one passed on from her father. On his death in 1952, she inherited the Beckhampton stables in Wiltshire, the racehorse stud at Sandringham and a string of thoroughbred racehorses. In the 70 years since, the Queen has become one of the world's most successful and knowledgeable owners and breeders, supported for 30 years by her racing manager and close friend, the Earl of Carnarvon. Following his death in 2001, this crucial role has been taken by his son John Warren.

Jockeys riding the Queen's colours are distinctive in their purple and scarlet jackets, complete with gold braiding, and no other owner is more elated in victory and quicker to the paddock when they come in first. This has been a frequent event down the years, with horses owned by the Queen winning over 1,600 races, including wins in all five Classics, including the Oaks in 1977, her Silver Jubilee year. So far, the one victory to elude her is that of the Epsom Derby, but it is not for want of trying. If she finally succeeds in the year of her Platinum Jubilee, her staff should probably order some extra copies of the Racing Post.

Above: Arriving in style at Royal Ascot, 16 days after the coronation
Left: The Queen is hands on at the races, 1953

HARVEYS

N#1 SHERRY

for the facts
drinkaware.co.uk

THE ILLUSTRATED
LONDON NEWS.

THE ROYAL TOUR

NEW SOUTH WALES

TASMANIA

VICTORIA

SOUTH AUSTRALIA

QUEENSLAND

WESTERN AUSTRALIA

CEYLON

UGANDA

MALTA

BERMUDA

AUSTRALIA

JAMAICA

FIJI

NEW ZEALAND

COVER GIRL

The unique archive of the Illustrated London News and its sister titles provides vivid,
exclusive coverage of the Queen in the public and private aspects of her extraordinary reign

The TATLER

Vol. CV. No. 1361.　　　London, July 27, 1927　　　POSTAGE: Inland 2d.; Canada and Newfoundland 1½d.; Foreign 4d.　　Price One Shilling.

Marcus Adams, Dover Street, W.

H.R.H. THE DUCHESS OF YORK AND THE PRINCESS ELIZABETH

A recent and quite exclusive portrait of two of the most popular ladies in the land, one of whom might some day be Queen of England. Since T.R.H. the Duke and Duchess of York's return from their great tour in Australia and New Zealand they have not been permitted to be exactly idle—no Royal personages ever are for long—and one of their recent engagements has been a visit to the great Advertising Exhibition at Olympia, where, amongst other things, the last word in perambulators greatly interested the Duke

c

For a woman so determinedly unshowy and self-contained, the Queen must surely be bemused by her status as one of the world's most photographed figures, but it is all she has ever known. From the day she was born, her every public move has been documented by the press, and none more affectionately than the Illustrated London News. Founded in 1842 as the world's first illustrated newspaper, the ILN shares with its sister titles a unique archive that reflects decades of special access to court events, state occasions and more intimate family gatherings.

The pictures in this extraordinary collection capture her earliest days as a young carefree princess, her marriage and motherhood, as well as her accession to the throne at a far younger age than anyone expected. From the pomp and splendour of the 1953 coronation to exotic trips all over the world as well as glimpses of her down-to-earth family life, the ILN's archive covers every aspect of her life in rich and rewarding detail. As such a unique and enduring subject, it is no surprise that Her Majesty has appeared on more front covers of the ILN, The Tatler, Bystander and The Sphere than anyone else in British history.

Opposite: The Illustrated London News Royal Tour 1953 issue marks that year's six-month royal tour for the Queen and the Duke of Edinburgh

Clockwise above:
The Tatler front cover featuring a photograph of the Duchess of York with Princess Elizabeth taken in July 1927, shortly after her first birthday; The Sphere celebrates the Queen's visit to Canada and the United States in 1957; The Sketch depicts Princess Elizabeth working for the ATS in 1945

Left: The Tatler magazine celebrates the coronation of Queen Elizabeth II in June 1953

the royal babies

Volume CCXXIII No. 2905

The SPHERE, London, October 15, 1955

The SPHERE

with which is
incorporated
THE GRAPHIC

Opposite clockwise: Princess Elizabeth of York aged two in 1928; The Queen and Prince Philip with their children Charles and Anne, 1959; The Queen with Princess Anne at King's Cross Station, 1955; Princess Elizabeth and Philip Mountbatten before their wedding, 1947; Princess Elizabeth attending the Trooping of the Colour, 1947; The Tatler features the Queen with her two younger children, Andrew and Edward, 1964
Above: The Queen with children Charles and Anne in Scotland, 1955

HOME SWEET HOMES

The Queen splits her time between four main residences across the United Kingdom, with each of them having a special place in her heart

WINDSOR CASTLE

Windsor Castle has been a royal home and fortress for nearly a thousand years, yet remains a working royal residence and the largest occupied castle in the world. In 1992, the Queen's "annus horribilis" included a fire that destroyed some of the building's most historic parts.

For many years, Windsor was where the Queen spent her weekends away from the capital, but the lockdown restrictions of 2020 saw the monarch decamp to Windsor full-time, and it was where the Duke of Edinburgh spent his final days. It has long provided a stunning backdrop for hosting state visits from overseas monarchs and presidents, as well as the annual Order of the Garter ceremony at St George's Chapel.

Many royal weddings have taken place in this intimate chapel, including those of the Prince of Wales and Duchess of Cornwall, the Duke and Duchess of Sussex and Princess Eugenie and Jack Brooksbank. In April 2021, it was the setting for the Duke of Edinburgh's funeral. With the spring sunlight shining on the ancient walls, Windsor Castle had never looked more majestic.

Left: The royal family in the East Terrace Garden of Windsor Castle, where the Queen has spent most weekends throughout her reign
Above: The Queen moved full-time to Windsor during the lockdown of 2020

entertaining, and when the Grand Ballroom (the Palace's largest room, at over 36 metres long) is prepared for state banquets, the Queen likes to inspect the table herself.

At the rear of the palace is London's largest private garden, where thousands of people gather for summer parties. Whether for dinners, lunches, receptions or other gatherings, around 50,000 guests receive an invitation to Buckingham Palace each year.

BALMORAL CASTLE

Ever since Queen Victoria, whose husband Prince Albert purchased this Scottish castle and grounds for her in 1852, described Balmoral in her journals as her "dear Paradise in the Highlands", the royal family has enjoyed an enduring affection for Balmoral. For many years, the Queen has based herself for August and September at the castle situated near the River Dee in Aberdeenshire, with many other family members making the same journey north during the summer holiday period.

There, they can enjoy undisturbed outdoor life, riding, fishing and wandering across the estate of 50,000 acres of heather-clad hills and ancient Caledonian woodland, or inspecting the herds of deer, Highland cattle and ponies. While the castle itself was rebuilt in the 1850s, Victoria committed to maintaining and preserving the landscape and wildlife around, and her descendants have followed suit, with the Duke of Edinburgh enlarging flower and vegetable gardens. While some guests, including several prime ministers and their spouses, have been daunted by the prospect of an invitation to the Queen's highland retreat, Balmoral remains one of the royal family's most beloved spots.

BUCKINGHAM PALACE

No postcard from London is complete without a picture of the most famous of the Queen's residences, this centrepiece of Britain's constitutional monarchy. The balcony at the front, overlooking the Queen Victoria Memorial and The Mall, must surely be the most recognisable in the world.

The Palace is both the administrative headquarters of the monarch and the official London residence of all British sovereigns since 1837. With 775 rooms built around a huge courtyard, there is ample space for the offices of staff supporting the day-to-day activities and duties of the Queen, as well as for royal ceremonies and investitures. The State Rooms are used by members of the royal family for official

Top: The front of Buckingham Palace, the administrative home of the monarchy, viewed from St James's Palace
Above: Balmoral, with its 100-foot clock tower, was first bought for Queen Victoria by Prince Albert.

SANDRINGHAM HOUSE

Sandringham House in Norfolk has been the private residence of four generations of sovereigns since 1862, when Queen Victoria purchased the property as a home for the Prince of Wales, the future Edward VII, and his new bride, Princess Alexandra.

The present Queen's attachment to the house and 20,000-acre estate has remained as strong as that of her ancestors, including her father, George VI, who died there in 1952, as had her grandfather George V in 1936. Sandringham was where the latter had made the first ever Christmas broadcast in 1932, and the Queen made history herself with the first ever televised version coming from the library in 1957.

Sandringham is the official Christmas base for the royal family, while the Queen remains in residence until February each year. After his retirement from public duties in 2017, the Duke of Edinburgh made nearby Wood Farm his base, and the Duke and Duchess of Cambridge's country residence Anmer Hall is also on the estate. Their daughter Princess Charlotte was christened at the Church of St Mary Magdalene in nearby Sandringham village.

Top: Sandringham House in Norfolk has become the royal family's traditional Christmas residence

Above: The Queen chose to spend 6 February 2022, the 70th anniversary of her accession, at Sandringham, where her father died in 1952

A UNIQUE REIGN,
AN EXTRAORDINARY LIFE

As the nation celebrates the Platinum Jubilee of our longest-reigning monarch, we look back on some of the most significant events in the life of Queen Elizabeth II

11 DECEMBER 1936
EDWARD VIII ABDICATES AND HIS BROTHER BECOMES KING GEORGE VI, PLACING ELIZABETH NEXT IN LINE FOR THE THRONE

When Princess Elizabeth was born at 2.40am on 21 April 1926 at 17 Bruton Street in London's Mayfair, there appeared to be little chance of her ever ascending the throne, with her uncle David seemingly destined to rule and pass the throne down through his line. But the shocking abdication of Edward VIII, determined to marry twice-divorced American socialite Wallis Simpson, resulted in a constitutional crisis and saw the destiny of the young princess change forever.

In the space of just 12 months, from January to December 1936, three monarchs occupied the throne. In rapid succession there occurred the death of Elizabeth's grandfather, George V, the short reign of her uncle, and finally the accession of her father, George VI. The new King stated that it was a "time of great distress" for him, yet despite his reluctance he set about fulfilling his role dutifully, famously promising to "uphold the honour of the Realm". For 10-year-old Elizabeth, the spotlight was now firmly upon her and her life became one of preparation for the throne.

Above right: Princess Elizabeth of York at the age of 14 months in June 1927
Below right: A group photograph of members of the royal family, taken after the christening of Princess Elizabeth at Buckingham Palace on 5 June 1926. Back row, left to right: the Duke of Connaught, King George V, the Duke of York, the Earl of Strathmore. Front row, left to right: Lady Elphinstone, Queen Mary, the Duchess of York with Princess Elizabeth, the Countess of Strathmore, Princess Mary

1920s

21 APRIL 1926
Princess Elizabeth Alexandra Mary is born at 17 Bruton Street, London (right)

29 MAY 1926
Archbishop of York, Cosmo Lang, baptises Elizabeth in the Private Chapel of Buckingham Palace

NOVEMBER 1928–MAY 1929
Regular visits from the little Princess are credited with helping the recovery of her grandfather, King George V, from serious illness

1930s

1930s Princess Elizabeth is educated at home, not at school

21 AUGUST 1930
Elizabeth's younger sister Princess Margaret Rose is born at Glamis Castle in Scotland

11 DECEMBER 1936
Edward VIII abdicates and his brother becomes King George VI, making Elizabeth next in line for the throne

1937 Princess Elizabeth becomes a Girl Guide at 11 years old

THE PRINCESS ANNE WITH HER MOTHER

THE ILLUSTRATED LONDON NEWS

Left: Princess Elizabeth making her first radio broadcast on 11 October 1940 to British children evacuated abroad

Above: Princess Anne in the arms of her mother at Clarence house, before her christening in October 1950; the Queen holding Prince Charles at his christening in December 1948

1940s

OCTOBER 1940 With Britain at war, Princess Elizabeth records her first public broadcast, a message for the children of Britain

21 APRIL 1942 Princess Elizabeth's first public engagement, on her 16th birthday, when she inspected the Grenadier Guards regiment

1945 Princess Elizabeth trains as a subaltern in the Auxiliary Territorial Service (left)

20 NOVEMBER 1947 Princess Elizabeth marries Philip Mountbatten, who becomes Duke of Edinburgh

14 NOVEMBER 1948 Prince Charles is born

20 NOVEMBER 1947
PRINCESS ELIZABETH MARRIES PHILIP MOUNTBATTEN, WHO BECOMES DUKE OF EDINBURGH

Prince Philip, Duke of Edinburgh, was born a Prince of Greece and Denmark in Corfu. He and Elizabeth met for the first time in 1934 at a wedding, then again in 1939 at the Royal Naval College in Dartmouth. They are said to have fallen in love soon afterwards, exchanging letters accordingly. The public announcement of their relationship and subsequent engagement were not without controversy, as Philip had no financial standing and was foreign-born. Elizabeth's mother was reported in early biographies to have opposed the union initially, seeing Philip as unsuitable, but in later life she commented that he was "an English gentleman".

The royal wedding took place in Westminster Abbey. In keeping with post-war austerity, the decorations and arrangements could not compare with previous state occasions, yet the number of people who assembled in London to show their loyalty was huge. Across the world, some 200 million people tuned in to listen to the event on the radio. By the time of the Duke's death in April 2021, the couple had been married for 73 years, enjoying a partnership that withstood family difficulties and was the longest of any reigning monarch in history.

Clockwise: Princess Elizabeth and the Duke of Edinburgh on their wedding day; the Archbishop of Canterbury places St Edwards crown on the Queen's head at her coronation; The Sphere and The Illustrated London News celebrate the coronation; Princess Elizabeth and the Duke of Edinburgh mark their wedding with a formal group photograph

1950s

15 AUGUST 1950 Princess Anne is born

6 FEBRUARY 1952 Elizabeth accedes to the throne, following the death of her father George VI

2 JUNE 1953 Coronation of Queen Elizabeth II at Westminster Abbey, the first televised coronation

1951 Princess Elizabeth tours Canada (pictured right meeting train porters)

1953 The Queen's sister, Princess Margaret falls in love with a divorced man, Group Capt Peter Townsend, prompting the royal family to veto their relationship – the first of several episodes of marital trouble during the Queen's reign

1953-1954
ACCESSION AND CORONATION

The sudden death of King George VI meant Queen Elizabeth II found herself on the British throne at the age of 25. She and her family moved into Buckingham Palace and prepared for the coronation to take place on 2 June 1953. The ceremony in Westminster Abbey was televised for the first time, and 27million Britons tuned in, many purchasing a television set to do so. Norman Hartnell's gown for the new monarch included embroidered floral emblems representing the countries of the Commonwealth.

1960s

19 FEBRUARY 1960
Prince Andrew is born

12 MAY 1961 Queen Elizabeth and the Duke of Edinburgh visit Pope John XXIII in Rome

10 MARCH 1964 Prince Edward (pictured right in 1965) is born

16 OCTOBER 1965 The Beatles receive MBEs from the Queen

1 JULY 1969 The Queen officially makes Prince Charles her successor by granting him the title of Prince of Wales (left)

21 JULY 1969 The Queen sends a message of congratulations to the Apollo 11 astronauts on the first moon landing

1977
CELEBRATIONS FOR QUEEN ELIZABETH II'S SILVER JUBILEE

The nation joined in celebrations to mark the Silver Jubilee in 1977, with a host of events held across the United Kingdom, from large-scale celebrations and parades to informal residential parties. The Queen herself embarked on a worldwide tour, but the key festivities centred on the "Jubilee Days" from 6th to 9th June, which coincided with Her Majesty's official birthday. Proceedings started with the Queen lighting a bonfire beacon at Windsor Castle, triggering a chain of beacons across the country.

The following day an estimated one million people turned out to watch the Gold State Coach travel to St Paul's Cathedral for a service of thanksgiving attended by the world's leading political figures and heads of state. Meanwhile, thousands of street parties to mark the occasion were held up and down the country. On 9th June, the Queen and Prince Philip took to the Thames for a traditional barge procession – travelling from Greenwich to Lambeth, with Her Majesty stopping to open the Silver Jubilee Walkway and the South Bank Jubilee Gardens. The procession culminated in a spectacular firework display, with the Queen returning to Buckingham Palace for a final appearance on the balcony. The celebrations reaffirmed Elizabeth's popularity and achieved her aim of uniting the nation.

Above: The Queen chats with crowds of well-wishers on a royal walkabout in London, part of her Silver Jubilee celebrations in 1977
Left: A group of children have a party in Horley, Surrey, one of thousands of events across the nation marking the Queen's 25th anniversary on the throne

1970s

5 JUNE 1972
The funeral of the Queen's uncle, The Duke of Windsor (formerly Edward VIII) takes place

14 NOVEMBER 1973
Princess Anne marries Capt Mark Phillips

20 OCTOBER 1973
The spectacular Sydney Opera House in Australia is officially opened by Queen Elizabeth II

1977 Celebrations for Queen Elizabeth II's Silver Jubilee are held, and depicted by the *ILN* (right)

15 NOVEMBER 1977
Princess Anne gives birth to Peter, the first of the Queen's eight grandchildren

27 AUGUST 1979 Earl Mountbatten of Burma, Prince Philip's uncle, is murdered by the IRA

Clockwise: The Prince of Wales marries Lady Diana Spencer, July 1981; the Queen's 'annus horribilis' in 1992 includes a fire at Windsor Castle; the Queen and Duke of Edinburgh inspect the thousands of bunches of flowers left outside Buckingham Palace following Diana's death, 1997

1990s
AN "ANNUS HORRIBILIS" AND DEATH OF PRINCESS DIANA

The Nineties presented the Queen with a catalogue of personal disasters. In 1992, her daughter Princess Anne divorced her first husband, Captain Mark Phillips, while both her elder sons also separated from their wives. On 21 November of that year, the monarch was pictured looking distraught as she inspected the damage the day after a fire destroyed much of the ancient parts of her beloved Windsor Castle. Three days later, even the normally reticent Queen used the occasion of a speech at London's Guildhall to reflect on a year she termed her "annus horribilis", and it was certainly challenging.

Five years later came a tragedy that would forever affect the royal family. In August 1997, Diana, Princess of Wales, was killed in a car accident in Paris, sparking an outpouring of grief from the British public never seen before. While the Queen remained at Balmoral and concentrated on supporting her bereaved grandsons, her reserve was seen as coldness and her initial response to the news found wanting. After several days, the Queen returned to Buckingham Palace where she inspected the thousands of flowers and tributes to Diana laid at the gates, and later paid warm and personal tribute to her former daughter-in-law.

1980s		1990s		
29 JULY 1981 Prince Charles marries Lady Diana Spencer	**21 APRIL 1986** Queen Elizabeth II celebrates her 60th birthday	**APRIL 1992** Princess Anne and Capt Mark Phillips divorce and she marries Cdr Timothy Laurence in the same year	**FEBRUARY 1993** The Queen begins paying taxes to assuage public sentiment against the state subsidising the throne	**30 MAY 1996** Duke and Duchess of York divorce
21 JUNE 1982 Charles and Diana's son Prince William is born	**23 JULY 1986** Prince Andrew marries Lady Sarah Ferguson	**20 NOVEMBER 1992** Fire destroys most of Windsor Castle	**20 DECEMBER 1995** The Queen urges Charles and Diana to divorce	**31 AUGUST 1997** Princess Diana is killed in a car crash in Paris
9 JULY 1982 Intruder breaks into the Queen's bedroom, she talks with him until police arrive		**9 DECEMBER 1992** Prince Charles and Princess Diana announce they are separating	**28 AUGUST 1996** Prince Charles and Princess Diana's final divorce decree is granted	**19 JUNE 1999** The Queen's son Edward, Earl of Wessex, marries Sophie Rhys-Jones, and they become the Earl and Countess of Wessex
15 SEPTEMBER 1984 Prince Harry is born				

2000s
THE GOLDEN JUBILEE AND A FAIRYTALE ROYAL WEDDING

The fortunes of the Queen and her family bounced back in the new millennium as the Queen Mother reached her 100th birthday in 2000, receiving a hand-written telegram from Buckingham Palace to mark the occasion. The Queen celebrated 50 years on the throne in 2002 and took the opportunity to thank the people for their support and loyalty during her reign, visiting 70 cities and towns across the United Kingdom over 38 days in the Golden Jubilee year.

In 2005, the Prince of Wales married for the second time, with his bride Camilla Parker Bowles becoming the Duchess of Cornwall. As the decade progressed, Queen Elizabeth II reached a number of other milestones. She celebrated her 80th birthday on 21 April 2006, and then marked her 60th wedding anniversary with the Duke of Edinburgh the following year. The royal couple marked the latter occasion by returning to the island of Malta, where they had lived for several extended periods between 1949 and 1951, before Elizabeth's accession to the throne.

From top: The Queen celebrates her Golden Jubilee in 2002; Prince Charles marries Camilla Parker Bowles at St George's Chapel, Windsor in 2005; HM The Queen Mother celebrates her 100th birthday on the balcony of Buckingham Palace

2000s

4 AUGUST 2000
The Queen Mother celebrates her 100th birthday

9 FEBRUARY 2002
Princess Margaret, the Queen's sister, dies at the age of 71

30 MARCH 2002
The monarch's mother Elizabeth, the Queen Mother, dies at 101

2002 Celebrations for the Queen's Golden Jubilee

8 NOVEMBER 2003
The Earl and Countess of Wessex have a baby girl named Lady Louise Windsor

9 APRIL 2005 Prince Charles marries Mrs Camilla Parker Bowles; the Queen does not attend their civil wedding but joins

the religious blessing service afterward

21 APRIL 2006 Queen Elizabeth II celebrates her 80th birthday

20 NOVEMBER 2007 Queen Elizabeth II and Prince Phillip mark their 60th wedding anniversary in Malta where they lived for two years at the start of their married life

2010s

29 APRIL 2011
Prince William marries Catherine Middleton and the Queen gives them the titles of the Duke and Duchess of Cambridge

17-20 MAY 2011
Queen Elizabeth II is the first UK monarch to visit the Republic of Ireland

JUNE 2012
Queen Elizabeth II celebrates her Diamond

2010s
THE DIAMOND JUBILEE AND THE BIRTH OF AN HEIR TO THE THRONE

The royal family experienced a resurgence of popularity in the 2010s. When Prince William married Catherine Middleton in Westminster Abbey in April 2011, it drew a reported global audience of 160 million and made headlines around the world.

The next year the nation rejoiced as London hosted the 2012 Olympics and the Queen celebrated her Diamond Jubilee. Celebrations included a river pageant on the Thames and a concert in front of Buckingham Palace.

The Duke and Duchess of Cambridge announced the birth of their first child, Prince George, in July 2013. Princess Charlotte followed in May 2015 and Prince Louis in April 2018. In May 2018, the Duke's brother Harry married Meghan Markle, the couple becoming the Duke and Duchess of Sussex. Their son Archie was born in May 2019 and their daughter Lilibet in June 2021.

2020s
FAMILY CHALLENGES, A GREAT LOSS AND THE QUEEN REACHES HER PLATINUM JUBILEE

With the 2020s arrived new trials for the Queen. In January 2020, her grandson and his wife, the Duke and Duchess of Sussex, announced their decision to step down as working royals. Like the rest of the world, the Queen's routine was thrown upside down by the arrival of the coronavirus and the ensuing lockdown restrictions. Her Majesty moved to Windsor Castle, from where she broadcast an uplifting national message in April 2020. The Duke of Edinburgh spent his last days at the Castle before his death in April 2021. The world watched the Queen grieve, sitting alone at his funeral in St George's Chapel.

As the Queen celebrates her Platinum Jubilee in 2022, some family members continue to present challenges from both sides of the Atlantic, but she presses on with plans for the future of the monarchy.

On 6 February this year, the 70th anniversary of her accession to the throne, Her Majesty expressed her wish that the Duchess of Cornwall be crowned Queen when her son Charles becomes King.

On that same day, she renewed her pledge to devote her life to the service of her subjects.

Above left: The Duke and Duchess of Cambridge with their children after the christening of Prince Louis in the Chapel Royal at St James's Palace in July 2018
Above: The Queen sits alone at the funeral of the Duke of Edinburgh in St George's Chapel, Windsor on 17 April 2021

ALAMY, SHUTTERSTOCK

2020s

Jubilee with a pageant on the River Thames and a concert in front of Buckingham Palace

27 JULY 2012
The Queen opens the Summer Olympics in London

9 SEPTEMBER 2015
The Queen becomes the longest-ever reigning British monarch, surpassing Queen Victoria

5 APRIL 2020
24 million people watch the Queen's message to her people, broadcast from Windsor Castle where she spends lockdown

9 APRIL 2021
HRH The Duke of Edinburgh dies two months short of his 100th birthday. The Queen reveals that his loss has "left a huge void"

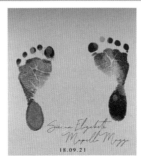
18.09.21

18 SEPTEMBER 2021
Princess Beatrice and her husband Edoardo announce the birth of their daughter Sienna, the Queen's twelfth great-grandchild

19 OCTOBER 2021
The Queen declines to accept The Oldie magazine's Oldie of the Year Award, explaining, "You're only as old as you feel"

6 FEBRUARY 2022
On the 70th anniversary of her Accession, the Monarch renews her pledge to serve her subjects for her whole life

2 TO 5 JUNE 2022
Four days of celebrations will include public events and national moments to reflect on the Queen's 70 years of service

Her Majesty's
Bon Mots

While she is famously discreet, the Queen has made many significant statements during the course of her 70 years on the throne, some of which have already gone down in history

ON HER REIGN

"I have in sincerity pledged myself to your service, as so many of you are pledged to mine. Throughout all my life and with all my heart I shall strive to be worthy of your trust."

(Coronation, 1953)

"With the benefit of historical hindsight we can all see things which we would wish had been done differently or not at all."

(State visit to Ireland, 2011)

ON THE COMMONWEALTH

"I cannot lead you into battle. I do not give you laws or administer justice but I can do something else. I can give my heart and my devotion to these old islands and to all the peoples of our brotherhood of nations."

(Christmas, 1957)

"Across continents and oceans, we have come to represent all the rich diversity of humankind."

(Commonwealth Day, 2009)

ON THE DEATH OF PRINCESS DIANA

"What I say to you now, as your Queen and as a grandmother, I say from my heart..."

"I for one believe that there are lessons to be drawn from her life and from the extraordinary and moving reaction to her death. I share in your determination to cherish her memory."

(Address to the nation, 1997)

ON FAITH AND THE CHURCH

"I, like so many of you, have drawn great comfort in difficult times from Christ's words and example."

(Christmas, 2000)

"The wellbeing and prosperity of the nation depend on the contribution of individuals and groups of all faiths and none."

(General Synod, 2005)

ON SOCIETY

"The upward course of a nation's history is due in the long run to the soundness of heart of its average men and women."

(Christmas, 1954)

"When life seems hard, the courageous do not lie down and accept defeat; instead, they are all the more determined to struggle for a better future."

(Christmas, 2010)

ON MEMBERS OF HER FAMILY

"He has, quite simply, been my strength and stay all these years."

(Paying tribute to the Duke of Edinburgh on their golden wedding anniversary, 1997)

"When, in the fullness of time, my son Charles becomes King, I know you will give him and his wife Camilla the same support that you have given me; and it is my sincere wish that, when that time comes, Camilla will be known as Queen Consort as she continues her own loyal service."

(February 2022)

IN RECENT TIMES

"I was blessed that in Prince Philip I had a partner willing to carry out the role of consort and unselfishly make the sacrifices that go with it."

(February 2022)

"We should take comfort that, while we may have more still to endure, better days will return: we will be with our friends again; we will be with our families again; we will meet again."

(Address to the nation during lockdown, April 2020)

"As I look forward to continuing to serve you with all my heart, I hope this Jubilee will bring together families and friends, neighbours and communities – after some difficult times for so many of us – in order to enjoy the celebrations and to reflect on the positive developments in our day-to-day lives that have so happily coincided with my reign."

(70th anniversary of accession to the throne, February 2022)